W I T

Praise for *The Top 50 Qu̶̶̶̶̶ ̶̶̶ ̶̶̶ Kids Ask*
(3rd through 5th Grade)

"If you've ever been stumped by a question your child has asked you, this book will help. Dr. Bartell identifies the 'hot-button' questions that consistently come up and actually provides the best possible answers to those questions so parents don't have to come up with them on their own on the spur of the moment."

—Elisa Ast All, cofounder, iParenting Media, and
executive editor of Disney Mom & Family Portfolio

"Finally, a book that answers all those questions we parents go in a cold sweat about! Dr. Susan tackles the tough ones such as money, shyness, siblings, and religion. Plus, we get the psychology behind it all to better understand our kids. You'll find yourself using this book every day."

—Pam Atherton, journalist and host of
A Closer Look radio talk show

"Tremendous, reassuring wisdom in an easy to access format!"

—Grace Housholder, editor of *Great Fort Wayne
(Indiana) Family* magazine

"Bill Cosby was correct—kids do say the darndest things. They also ask the darndest questions. What a stroke of brilliance to have captured these questions and then to provide parents with the best way to respond to each. Dr. Susan Bartell has once again found a way to offer sensible, succinct, and straightforward advice in yet another amazing book."

> —Sara Dimerman, Psych. Assoc., child and
> family therapist, author of *Character Is
> the Key* and *Am I a Normal Parent?*

"Dr. Susan is highly gifted at helping parents and kids connect from the heart. This book honors our innate wisdom, supports us in nurturing our kids' emotional growth, and empowers us to be the parents we were meant to be."

> —Renee Peterson Trudeau, life balance
> expert/coach and author of *The Mother's
> Guide to Self-Renewal: How to Reclaim,
> Rejuvenate and Re-Balance Your Life*

"If you value good sense, and you need some advice that works—in the heat of a tricky moment with your kid and long-term, too—this is the parenting guide for you."

> —Sarah Smith, editor-in-chief of *Kiwi* magazine

"Dr. Susan Bartell has done it again! She takes the toughest questions that kids ask us parents and gives us clear steps to figure out how we'll answer *before* the questions are asked. Using her recommendations will deepen communication and understanding between children and parents."

—Nancy Gruver, founder of New Moon Girl Media and author of *How to Say It to Girls*

"Easy-to-implement parenting advice in bite-sized, easy-to-read pieces. Dr. Bartell states the question, uncovers the meaning, and suggests how to respond."

—Lucy Banta, managing editor of *New Jersey Family* and *Raising Teens*

THE TOP 50
Questions
KIDS ASK

• 3rd through 5th Grade •

THE TOP 50 Questions
KIDS ASK

• 3rd through 5th Grade •

The Best Answers
to the Smartest,
Strangest, and
Most Difficult
Questions Kids
Always Ask

DR. SUSAN BARTELL

sourcebooks

Published by Sourcebooks, Inc.
P.O. Box 4410, Naperville, Illinois 60567-4410
(630) 961-3900
Fax: (630) 961-2168
www.sourcebooks.com

Library of Congress Cataloging-in-Publication Data

Bartell, Susan.
  The top 50 questions kids ask (3rd through 5th grade) : the best answers to the smartest, strangest, and most difficult questions kids always ask / Susan Bartell.
    p. cm.
  1. Children's questions and answers. I. Title.
HQ784.Q4B37 2010
649'.124—dc22

                    2009039240

For my children, Max, Gillian, and Mollie.
You started asking questions as soon as you
could talk, and I hope you never stop!

For every child and parent with
whom I have ever worked.
Your questions have taught me how to help
kids be happy, and I am deeply grateful.

Contents

Acknowledgments

This book could not have been written without the hundreds and hundreds of questions that were submitted by parents from every state and from countries as far away as England and Australia, and as close as Jamaica and Canada. I thank each one of you for responding to my request for questions and even more so for forwarding my request to other moms and dads. Your children's questions really were a window into your lives—some made me cry, others let me see the exasperation that all kids can evoke, and a few were so funny I laughed until I cried. Whether or not I used your question, each submission helped to inform and shape my writing, so you have my deepest gratitude.

Once again, I want to thank my editor at Sourcebooks, Sara Appino. This is our second project together, and

Sara continues to prove herself to be insightful, clear-thinking, and hard-working. I appreciate her advocacy of my work and her enthusiastic personality.

As with every book I write, I consider having the opportunity to write a luxury that I wouldn't have been able to achieve without the support of my family. My children, Max, Gillian, and Mollie, are my constant cheering team—I couldn't be a luckier mom, and I love you to the moon, to the stars, to Brooklyn, and back again.

My parents and my mother-in-law, aside from telling me (and anyone else who will listen) how proud they are of me, offer consistent, practical help with anything and everything—whenever I ask. I am truly grateful to have your support, and I love you.

If you know me at all, you will realize that my last thank-you always goes to my husband Lewis. This is because if I started with him, there wouldn't be space for anyone else on the page. We always work together as a team to support each other's important life projects, and this one is no exception. Lew, I don't have the words to thank you for your continued dedication to me and to our family. You are my never-ending love.

Susan Bartell, PsyD
March 2010

Introduction

If your child is anything like mine, questions are being fired at you constantly throughout the day, beginning with, "What can I have for breakfast?" with no end in sight until, "Can I stay up for ten more minutes?" I bet sometimes your child doesn't even wait for an answer to one question before moving on to the next one. And I'm sure that sometimes a single question is repeated so many times, it makes you want to scream. (After about the twentieth time asked, I actually think it's okay to scream, if for no other reason than simply to break the cycle of asking. I mean, you're only human, right?) But keep reading, because right away in Chapter One we'll talk about simple, easy ways to reduce—even eliminate—relentless, nagging questions.

The questions upper-elementary-age kids ask aren't

simply annoying and exhausting (although sometimes they are *very* much that). In fact, as they develop, older-elementary-age children very often ask questions as a way to let you know their concerns, interests, worries, and fears. The key is to really pay attention to your child's questions. As parents we often wish we could see into our children's minds, to know what they are thinking and feeling. By listening hard to your child's questions, you can very frequently do just that. You can even learn how to respond to certain questions in the right way so that you will encourage further important, intimate conversation, rather than shutting it down. Throughout *The Top 50 Questions*, I will show you how to help your child turn one single question into an entire conversation about a topic that is worrying, frustrating, or confusing him. You can become an expert—as good as any psychologist—at getting your child to open up and talk about everything that is on his mind.

At this stage of development, your child is also beginning to flex some muscles of independence, and the questions she asks will reflect this. Therefore, some of your child's questions will be feisty and challenging, making you wonder what happened to your sweet little one. But this is a natural part of growing up. As your child becomes a "big kid" in school, she also starts to feel confident enough to stand up to you once in a while—and question your authority in small ways. By responding to her challenging questions smoothly, rather than antagonistically, you will find that your relationship with your child will continue to grow stronger and more intimate, rather than becoming locked in friction.

You'll be interested to know that the questions in *The Top 50 Questions* are all *real* questions from parents *just like you*, from all over the United States and even other parts of the world. In fact, I received hundreds and hundreds of questions in response to an online request that I generated. You're probably wondering how I decided which questions to include and which ones to leave out. Actually, it was quite a simple decision. Just as there are predictable physical growth patterns that occur during the later elementary years, the emotional changes in your child's life will also take a predictable path, and this will be reflected in the types of questions he or she asks. Based on this, many of the submissions I received from parents had similar responses. In fact, I very seriously considered naming this book *"What's for Dinner?" and 49 Other Questions Kids Ask*, since this was, by far, the most commonly submitted question by parents of upper-elementary-age kids.

The selection process for *The Top 50 Questions* was based on which questions I received most frequently from parents with children in the third to fifth grade range. It was that simple—and that complicated. I have to admit, there were some questions that I absolutely loved—they made me laugh, cry, or think really hard, but because they didn't reflect the norm, I couldn't include them. But if you submitted questions, and now you are reading this book and don't see your child's question, don't think for a second I didn't consider yours. I read each and every question, and struggled mightily with which ones to include. Every question touched me.

As with physical growth, the range of "normal" for emotional, social, cognitive, and academic growth is huge, which is why *The Top 50 Questions* covers third all the way through fifth grade—one child may ask a question in third grade, but another child may not be ready to ask the very same question until fifth grade. Both are normal, regular kids. In fact, if you haven't read it yet, I definitely suggest you pick up *The Top 50 Questions Kids Ask (Pre-K through 2nd Grade)*. It's a great basis for this book, even if you don't have a child in that age range any more. You'd be surprised how many older kids are still asking questions from their earlier years. So it would be wonderful for you not only to understand why your child is asking these questions, but to really know how to answer them in a way that would satisfy your child.

Of course, some children can actually be much less or much more sophisticated than their peers when it comes to asking questions or, in fact, any other area of emotional development. When this happens, a parent may begin worrying that a child's behavior seems to be too different from the way other children are behaving. If this seems to describe your child—if you have any concerns that your child is somehow "behind" or even too far ahead developmentally, cognitively, or socially—it's important not to ignore it. Speak to your child's medical doctor, your child's teacher, the school counselor, or a child psychologist or social worker. If there is a problem, then the earlier you address it, the better it is for your child—and for you.

By taking a quick glance at the Table of Contents, you will see that the questions are divided into nine chapters. I have chosen these chapters carefully to represent the most important areas of emotional and cognitive development for children in the upper elementary school grades. As you read *The Top 50 Questions*, these chapters will make sense to you. You will find yourself nodding in agreement as you see your child reflected in the questions (even if you didn't submit a single one of them). Then as you begin to understand the best ways to respond to each question, it will again make sense and will feel natural and easy for you. In fact, none of this is going to feel like hard work. Your child is asking you the questions anyway—you will simply need to learn how to tweak your responses so that you answer in a way that will actually strengthen and deepen your relationship with your child and also reduce your own frustration. By responding differently, you will begin to decrease the "nag, nag, nag" factor and understand your child just a little bit better than you did before you began reading. Sounds good, right? Well, I think we are ready to begin.

As always, I love to hear from those who read my books, so feel free to email me at DrSusan@DrSusanBartell. com. Send me more questions too, if you like, and maybe the next book will include yours.

Happy answering!

Dr. Susan

Nag, Nag, Nag

As your child's language grows more proficient, her ability to ask all types of questions greatly improves. However, along with this, her aptitude for nagging becomes more sophisticated as well—lucky you! The late elementary grades often represent the peak of the "nagging" years, because as your child becomes more involved in her social life, the influence of peers sways her to nag you for privileges and material items that prior to now she might not even have known existed.

An older child may also nag when she's angry with you. She knows that yelling at a parent is not socially appropriate and that you probably (hopefully) would not tolerate it. But at this age, she realizes that nagging will also push your buttons and drive you crazy (perhaps even more so!), just in a slightly less egregious manner.

Last, and perhaps most important, your child recognizes that nagging will often get her exactly what she wants—as long as she is persistent.

Now that you understand a little bit about how nagging works, let's take a look at the most frequently "nagged" questions, uncover their real meaning, and learn the very best responses to them. By the end of this chapter, you'll be an expert on nagging and how to get your child to do it less often—I promise.

#1: WHAT'S FOR DINNER?

As I explained in the introduction, this was the most frequently submitted of *all* questions. I received it from every corner of the country in a variety of versions. The submission that made me laugh the most came from Tara, mom of Alec and Christian (both age 9) and Eugenie (age 4). When she submitted the question, she added, "This question annoys me because of the look of disappointment they have on their faces before they even hear the answer." I still chuckle every time I read her comment!

So why do children ask this question over and over again, and what is the best strategy to respond to it in a way that might break the cycle?

Uncovering the Meaning

When your child asks this question, he could have one of several different agendas. Of course, off the top, it may just be sheer curiosity. But this is the least likely reason of all.

Like Tara's kids, he may want to ensure that he won't be disappointed by the meal selection. If he finds that he is disappointed, he wants to have ample time to begin a campaign to either change the night's menu or suggest an alternative. He likely realizes that getting you to prepare a second choice might take a great deal *more* nagging!

On a more serious note, your child may also ask the question as a way to check with you to see whether it is a "sit-down" night or a casual "take-out" night. In many busy homes the dinner meal is the only time that a family gathers to sit together, not only to eat but to share a few minutes of time at the end of a hectic day. Your child may feel that he does not get enough of these meals, but doesn't know how to articulate this. Instead, he prepares himself for another rushed dinner meal, by asking in advance, "What's for dinner?"

Another reason your child may ask this question is to gauge the level of order (or disorder) in your home. In some families, meals are flung together at the last minute, amid homework, activities, running around, and bath time. It can be disillusioning to a very hungry child to not know *what's* for dinner and also to not know *when* dinner will be offered. A child may ask this question over and over each day in an attempt to prompt the adult in charge to become motivated to push dinner preparation to the top of the priority list.

Since food—especially dinner—seems to be such an important issue, what is the best way to respond to this question? Jump right to the next section, and you'll find out.

The Best Way to Respond

One very easy way to alleviate your child's need to ask this question every day is to make a dinner menu for each night of the week. Children love routine, so as long as you and the rest of your family don't get bored, you can offer the same menu each week so your child knows exactly what to expect—no surprises. Post the menu in the kitchen for everyone to see.

I recommend preparing the menu with your child or children. Discuss the importance of eating healthily and making sure each meal includes enough protein and vegetables. Allow your child to offer suggestions for what meals should be included on the weekly menu—and make sure to include them.

If you tend to be a very busy, frequent fast-food family, with lots of eating on the run, try to cut back or at least opt for healthier fast foods, eaten together as a family. Fast food is one of the main contributors to overweight kids (and parents) in Western culture. If this is difficult for you to do, check out my book *Dr. Susan's Fit and*

Fun Family Action Plan. It will teach you exactly how to feed your kids more healthily.

In addition, studies show that when families eat together regularly, teens are significantly less likely to smoke, drink, and use drugs. Since it won't work to suddenly tell your teen that you want to start having family meals, *you need to start making it a family habit now* before your child reaches adolescence.

Many parents ask me whether they should give their children a choice or make them eat what has been prepared. If you have prepared a meal that you know your child enjoys (especially if he helped create the menu), then it is acceptable not to offer another choice—no matter how many times he nags. However, if you know your child doesn't like what you have prepared (or if two of your children like it but the third doesn't), I'd recommend offering that child another option. You don't have to make another full meal, but a sandwich, eggs, or even a bowl of cereal with fruit is a good alternative. No one forces adults to eat food they don't like, and I don't believe a child should be forced to do so either. The only exception to this is when you have a very picky eater who needs help learning to eat a larger variety of foods. In this case, your child needs frequent exposure to small amounts of one food at a time. This requires great patience on your part, but is well worth the effort.

If you've assessed that your child is asking this question because your home is chaotic and dinner time is erratic, it is time to make a change—not only for the sake of dinner, but because it is not healthy for your child to feel that his life is unpredictable and without order. Begin by assessing whether you and your child(ren) are juggling too many activities, whether you have competent child care, or perhaps whether you need to seek professional help to support the changes you want to make. Start to change by planning dinner for the same time every day. Perhaps you can cook and freeze some meals on the weekends; maybe you need to purchase easy-to-prepare foods like cut-up vegetables. Once you have dinner time running more smoothly, then move to the next area. Before you know it, you'll find that you have your home in better control and your child won't be asking this question nearly as often.

#2: CAN WE GET A DOG?
(OR: CAN WE GET A CAT? CAN I GET A HORSE?)

"Natalie (age 9) and Jackson (age 12) ask their father and me this question at least three times a week," offered their mother, Holly, shaking her head in resignation. "They promise they will do *everything* to take care of it. I've almost given in at least five times, but not quite yet. But I have to admit, I don't think I'll last much longer!"

Many pets have been purchased based on a child's well-intentioned promise that she will take care of it.

Pets have also been brought home because a child expresses interest, and a parent becomes convinced that it will be good for the child to have an animal to care for. How well does this work out? Let's explore the issue.

Uncovering the Meaning

Think back—do you remember thinking what it would be like to be a parent, how much fun it would be, that you would have the perfect child, that it would at all times be the most wonderful and joyful experience of your life? And then you became a parent for real. No one could have actually prepared you for it, right?

Just as you could not have begun to imagine what it was like to be a parent before your child arrived, your child can really only think about the "fun" part of owning a pet. This is true no matter how much you explain, prepare, and tell your child what it would *really* be like to have to take care of an animal.

She may spend the afternoon with a friend's pet and see how much fun it is and come home wanting one. She may even be a real animal lover and truly want one of her own.

Despite all of this, it is important for you to know that when a child wants a pet badly enough, she will promise you anything in order to get one—and she won't be fibbing at the time she makes the promise! She will truly believe that she will feed, walk, bathe, play with, and otherwise care for the dog, cat, or other animal.

But you also need to know that your child does not yet have the cognitive ability to really think well enough into the future, or to be self-reflective enough to know whether she has the ability to sustain this level of responsible behavior. You may want to believe her when she promises, with great conviction, that she will be supremely committed to the new pet. You may actually believe that she's capable of doing all that she is promising. But, when your child asks you this question again and again and again, and then makes all kinds of promises, the truth is that neither you nor your child can be sure that she is capable of actually following through on these promises.

She might be able to follow through, but it is also possible that you will be the one taking care of the new pet. This is something about which you need to be absolutely crystal clear before you give your child a response. So what is the best way to respond to this question?

The Best Way to Respond

Your response should depend on whether you want a pet and whether you would be willing to take care of it, assuming that your child completely fails to follow through on any of her promises.

If you are an animal lover and are happy to feed, walk, train, and otherwise take care of your new dog, then go right ahead and get one. Begin teaching your child how to care for the new pet by giving her age-appropriate pet-related duties, without overwhelming her (despite the fact that she may have promised to do everything). She is much more likely to be consistent in feeding the dog once a day or walking it twice on the weekends, than if she is expected to feed it twice a day or walk it every single day. By offering her a small task that she can complete, she will feel accomplished and you won't feel annoyed or disappointed.

However, if you are *not* an animal lover and you have no desire to feed, clean up after, train, pay for, or otherwise take care of a pet, it is imperative that you respond to your child's question each and every time by saying *no*.

I will reiterate that a child this age is not capable of taking full responsibility for a pet, and I assure you that at least part of this task will fall to you within days of the adorable animal entering your home. This will lead to stress, resentment, anger, and fights between you and your child. This is not the way to teach a child responsibility, nor is it fair to the animal that did not enter your home voluntarily. In addition, your child is certainly not capable of assuming the financial burden of having a pet. This is something you need to be willing to incur without any resentment toward your child.

A great way for both you and your child to "try out" the possibility of having a pet would be to borrow one from a friend for several days or longer and see how it feels to take care of it. I'd recommend "adopting" an animal from a friend or relative for more than just a weekend, so that the "honeymoon effect" will have a chance to wear off and your family can really see how it feels to take care of a pet.

#3: WHAT TIME ARE YOU COMING HOME? (OR: WHAT TIME IS DADDY COMING HOME?)

Hector's work hours are somewhat erratic. He explained, "Every single day after school, my kids, Angelo (age 8) and Edwin (age 6½), call me at work and start asking—or should I say nagging—when I will be home from work. Since I don't come home at exactly the same time every day, it's frustrating."

It can be distracting, feel like pressure, and, for some parents, induce feelings of guilt when you hear this particular nagging, whining question—usually over the phone, in a message left on your voicemail, or via text message or email. For some parents it also evokes sparks of resentment—usually when the question comes while you're trying to carve out a little bit of social or personal time.

If your child asks this question so often that it feels like nagging, there is a reason for it, so let's explore the different reasons and also the best possible ways to respond to your child.

Uncovering the Meaning

To begin, it is possible that your child is simply curious as to when you will be home, and there is nothing more to it than that. However, if your child keeps asking even after you have given an answer, this is not likely the reason he is asking.

Rather, your child may be asking because, like Hector, you have erratic hours and he is unsure when he will see you. This unpredictability can be disconcerting for a child. Not only does he want to have time with you, but he also may need help with homework, or to chat about social or other issues.

Although separation issues are less common in the older elementary grades, your child may have the remnants of one from earlier years, and this question could reflect his anxiety about being away from you for too long.

A child may also ask this question because he does not feel satisfied with the childcare provider with whom he has been left. The person could be too strict, unpleasant, or apathetic. Perhaps there is disorder when you're not home, or maybe siblings are mean to each other.

Another reason that your child may ask you this question frequently could be that you are out or away excessively. Do you work exceptionally long hours and frequently go out socially? Perhaps you are not spending enough time with your child. It can be difficult to be self-reflective enough to really take a good look at this issue. But if your child is very frequently asking you when or what time you will be home, it could be a "red flag" that you're not at home enough with your child.

The Best Way to Respond

One of the best ways to minimize the number of times this question is nagged at you is to tell your child when you will be home *before* he has a chance to ask. For example, each day, after school, make a quick call home and tell your child what time you expect to be home that day. If your estimate changes, call back and let him know. While this may seem inconvenient, it will go a long way toward building an excellent relationship with your child. Take a quick look into the future with me. When your child becomes a teen, if you expect him to tell you when he will be late coming home (and where he is), it is much more likely that he will do so if you show him the same respect for several years as he is growing up.

This technique also works well if your child has separation anxiety. Knowing your schedule will reduce his worry and free him to focus on things other than trying to figure out when you will be home.

If, while asking you when you will be home, your child also complains about the baby-sitter or the situation at home, it may be time to reassess your child care. A happy child is less likely to complain or to miss you while you are out. A child in the upper elementary grades can be an excellent reporter. Take the time to talk to your child in detail about how he likes the baby-sitter, what he thinks is positive and negative, and what makes him always ask what time you will be home and complain about you being away. Try to be objective about your childcare provider—particularly if it is a grandparent who takes care of your child or children. It may be a convenient situation for you, and it may have worked when your children were younger, but it may not be great any more. It is difficult to change childcare situations, but if your child's reasons for being unhappy are legitimate, it is time to reevaluate.

Last, if your child asks you this question frequently because, you recognize, you are out too much, then perhaps it is time to respond by saying, "I will be home very soon, and tomorrow night I am not going out at all. We will have the whole evening together. You can choose what we should do."

But how should you respond when your child asks this question no matter what—even though you spend a lot of time with him? All you want is a couple of hours alone or with friends, without being nagged to come home. In this case, respond with a variation of the following: "I'm out with my friends having fun, just like you get to do with your friends. I will be home in three hours. You are being taken care of, so please don't call me again. But if you do, I'm not going to answer my phone. If there's an emergency, you should leave me a message. I will check the message and call back. If it is a real emergency—for example, the baby-sitter collapses—you should call 911 before calling me. I love you, and I'll see you later." (This last bit of advice is important information to give to any child old enough to operate a phone.) Then hang up, and don't answer another call.

- -

#4: WHAT ARE WE DOING NEXT?
(OR: WHAT ARE WE DOING TODAY?)

- -

"Emma and Dylan (both 9) wake up every Saturday morning and ask, 'What are we doing today?'" reported their mother, Robin. "Then, throughout the day—and the weekend—they ask, 'What are we doing next?' It drives me crazy. It's as though it's never enough."

I hear this question everywhere. Not only was it one of the most commonly submitted questions, but I hear it as kids greet their parents after school, at the *end* of a busy day, while standing in line at the supermarket, yes, even in my very own kitchen from the mouths of my eleven-, thirteen-, and fifteen-year-old children.

Uncovering the Meaning

Many parents become exasperated when a child asks this question. It makes them feel like their child is ungrateful: "We've just finished a wonderful, fun-filled activity and she is asking, 'What's next?' I can't believe it!"

But the truth is, kids—even teens—do not ask this question because they are unappreciative of or undervalue the activity they just experienced. Rather, they do not yet have the ability to regulate their own intake of "fun and games." Therefore, once your child is feeling excited, she will want to continue this level of excitement, even if it isn't in her best interest. This will prompt her to ask, "What's next?" It is similar to a child wanting to stay up late even when she is exhausted. It is your job to help her calm down and realize that there doesn't have to be a "next" activity.

Sometimes a child will ask the question because you have scheduled many chores or mundane activities, but you haven't given her a schedule. Her question is simply to try and get a plan for what her day will look like as the day unfolds. After all, she has little control over the day. Unless you tell her, she needs to keep asking.

Your child may ask you the question, "What are we doing today?" for a similar reason. For example, if you are not a family that plans activities in advance, your child may ask in order to force you to think about organizing your day. Perhaps she doesn't want to spend the whole day doing nothing—especially on a weekend day. By asking you the question, she probably thinks that there is a slightly better chance that you will do something, rather than doing nothing. Is she right? If she is, you should probably use this nagging question as an indication that it is time to make a change.

The Best Way to Respond

This question often frustrates and annoys parents so much that their first response is to yell. So begin by taking a deep breath. Getting angry because you believe your child is unappreciative will not help her to understand that it is time to either focus on enjoying the activity in which she is engaged, or take some time to calm down and relax after completing an exciting activity. A response that would help your child to transition might be similar to the following: "We have had such a fun time today. Why don't you tell me three things that you really loved about what we just did? Then we will be going home to have dinner, have a bath, and it will be time for bed."

When your child frequently asks you at the beginning of the day for the day's agenda, it means it is time to share it with her. If you have a plan, tell your child what will be happening, in order. If you don't have a plan, make one with your child. It doesn't have to be detailed, but it should be anchored by one or two activities or chores so that she knows what to expect.

#5: WHERE IS MY_____ [FILL IN THE BLANK]?

"Mom, where is my sneaker/lacrosse stick/brush/math book/game/sneaker/pen/lunch box/baseball mitt/did I say sneaker? This is all I hear all day long from Austen and Drew (both age 10)." Cindi, the boys' mother, shook her head in exasperation. "I'm not sure how they get through the day without losing themselves!"

Why can't your child keep track of his belongings? It seems simple enough, doesn't it? But for so many kids, misplacing and outright losing their stuff is a constant battle, and the established pattern is that your child relies on you to find it for him. So where is that pesky sneaker?

Uncovering the Meaning

By the later elementary years, your child is old enough to keep track of his belongings, so why is he always nagging you to help him find them? There could be a few different reasons for this.

To begin, perhaps you make it too easy for him to rely on you because whenever he asks you this question, you immediately rush to help him look for the missing item, rather than insisting that he look for it himself.

It's also possible that you haven't taught him how to be organized, or maybe you don't role-model it in your home. Ask yourself the following questions. If you can't answer yes to most of them, you are not role-modeling an organized home environment for your child; it is therefore not surprising that he is always asking you this question.

- Is your home generally clean and tidy (no dishes piled in the sink, dirty laundry lying around, toys everywhere)?
- Is your home usually free of clutter (surfaces aren't piled up with papers and magazines)?

- Can you find your things when you need them?
- Do you pick up after yourself and teach your child to do the same?
- Do you put your belongings away and teach your child to do the same?

Even if your home is generally tidy and organized, it is possible that your child has difficulty in this area. Some children have a notable—even clinically diagnosable—problem with organization, which results in them not only losing things, but also forgetting to bring home schoolwork, having very messy rooms, desks, and school bags, and even having academic difficulties. The older elementary grades are very often the time that these difficulties are first seen in school. Therefore, if your child has trouble with losing things and with organization in all areas of his life, it is a good idea to speak to your child's teacher and to the school psychologist.

The Best Way to Respond

In all cases, it is important to make sure that your child's space is clutter-free and organized. Then, teach him the necessary skills to begin learning how *not* to lose his belongings. This includes making sure that he puts things away after using them and that he has an organized area to keep his things. It also means teaching him to look for things himself so he doesn't rely on you to do it for him.

He will be less likely to lose things carelessly if he knows that he will have to find them himself. The best response to this question is therefore a version of the following: "You need to look for your sneaker yourself. Think about where you last had it, and begin there. I'm sure when you look for a while you'll find it. Let me know when you do; I'll be in the den."

#6: CAN I GET A CELL PHONE?

Wendi and Greg are nagged relentlessly by Alyssa (age 9), who is apparently "dying" for a cell phone. And it seems they are not alone. Wendi explains, "Alyssa says that everyone has a phone except her. But that can't be true, because I know at least ten other nine-year-olds who don't have one yet, and plenty of older kids as well. I also know lots of kids her age who do have a cell phone, so I'm not sure when the best time is to give her one."

We live in an ever-advancing technological age and our kids are even more advanced than we are. So how do you best respond to this question? Is peer pressure a legitimate reason to give your child a cell phone, or should you be guided by something a little more scientific? Keep reading and you'll find out.

Uncovering the Meaning

For the most part, an elementary-school-age child's desire for a cell phone has very little to do with being practical and everything to do with being "cool." She desires a cell phone for one or more of the following reasons:

- An older sibling has a phone.
- Several of her friends have phones.
- It's another great piece of technology with fun games and ringtones.
- She wants to be in touch with her friends when she's not with them.

As long as you are aware that these are the reasons that your child wants a phone, it is not necessarily a bad idea to get her one, as long as you are doing it for a reason that is important to you and *not* for one of the above reasons. Does this sound strange? Let's keep going, and soon it will make sense.

No matter what your child's age, you do not need to give her a cell phone until you feel that it would be beneficial for her to have one. On the other hand, if you feel that having one at eight or nine years old would be helpful, then there is no need to wait. Some reasons that you may want to give your child a phone right now include the following:

- You work and your child is in an after-school program, and you want to be able to reach her during the day.

- She's alone on the bus for a short period of time, and knowing that she has a phone makes you more comfortable.
- She's on a travel sports team and you want her to be able to call you from away games.
- You frequently travel for work, and giving her a cell phone will make it easier for you to stay in touch with her when you're away.

The Best Way to Respond

As you can see, I do not believe that there are hard and fast rules for how to respond to this question. You should give your child a phone when it is best for you and your family that your child should have a phone. We live in a technologically sophisticated time, and there is no reason for you or your child not to take advantage of this. Indeed, pay phones are scarce, and no one even knows how to use them anymore.

However, along with the privilege of a cell phone comes the responsibility. So, much as you give your child rules about crossing the street and about Internet safety, once you answer this question by saying, "Yes, you can get a cell phone," it is important to teach your child that the cell phone comes with rules, including the following:

- Do not give your number to anyone you don't know.
- Do not download anything to your phone without permission (this requires giving out your number).

- Only call and text as often as your parents allow you to—going over the allotted minutes should result in a consequence.
- Never use your phone during school hours, unless it is an emergency.

It is also important to understand that giving a child a cell phone can change the way she interacts with the people in her world. It is your job to make sure that the phone doesn't have a negative effect on her social interactions or ability to be independent. For example, I have known homesick children who, while at a sleepover, have called their parents from their cell phones instead of telling the "sleepover" parents they are feeling homesick. While this seems okay on the surface, in reality it deprives that child of having to try to work through the homesickness with the adult in charge. I've also known children who call their parents from playground fights to ask for help.

When your child's cell phone offers her so much access to you that it interferes with her ability to work through the struggles of her everyday life—like a sleepover or an argument with a peer—the cell phone is harming rather than helping. In this case, you need to decide whether your child should have only limited access to her phone.

2

The World Outside

By third grade and above, your child is accustomed to school, and unless he is having a particular difficulty, his social and school lives have probably begun to take on a predictable rhythm. By now you are able to observe your child's personality and tell if he is outgoing or shy, slightly rigid or flexible, feisty or generally compliant. Each child is different from every other, and as your child grows—venturing away from home and exploring his world—these differences become more and more apparent.

One thing that most upper-elementary-age children tend to have in common with each other is that they begin to question everything. No longer is your child a "newbie" kindergartner or first-grader, unsure of herself and experiencing everything as brand-new. Instead, she may be more willing to challenge you, her friends, and possibly even a teacher. The questions she asks reflect this.

So hang on to your seat, because the preteen years are just around the corner, and the way you respond to your child's questions now will help determine the type of communication you establish with him, as well as the all-important boundaries you create, which will take him into the older years, when real limit-testing is much more likely.

Now, I am sure you are ready to examine your child's most pressing questions about his world and help him learn to negotiate his concerns as smoothly as possible. So let's go!

#7: WHY DO I HAVE TO DO LONG DIVISION/LEARN NAMES OF ROCKS/ MAKE ART WITH "FOUND OBJECTS"/ [FILL IN YOUR CHILD'S COMPLAINT] IF I DON'T NEED IT WHEN I'M A GROWN-UP?
(OR: WHY DO I HAVE TO DO HOMEWORK?)

Lucy's son Cheng (age 10½) gives her a hard time about school almost every day. Lucy says Cheng loves the social aspect of school and some of the academics, but he is very dismissive about some aspects of the learning process. "I'm not sure whether to laugh or be angry with Cheng when he makes comments to me like 'I don't see why I need to do this project; I'll never need to know about the pilgrims when I'm a grown-up,' or 'This is a waste of time. *You* use a calculator; why can't I?'"

Does this sound familiar to you? If it does, you are not alone, and neither is Lucy. Many older-elementary-age kids question why they have to learn certain topics, do homework, or even go to school at all. While these types of questions can be annoying to you, they are part of your child's emotional development. Let me explain.

Uncovering the Meaning

In asking a version of this question, your child is beginning to challenge the adult authority in her life. It might be disconcerting to hear me say this—you're thinking, "Dr. Susan, isn't this sort of behavior reserved for teens?"

In thinking back to the "olden days" when we were young, it feels like kids didn't begin questioning authority until they were much older—if ever! However, I'm not sure that this is entirely true. It might just be our revised recollection of our not-actually-perfect childhoods.

However, even if it is true, it is not fair to compare our children with ourselves all those years ago. Our children live in a complex world that expects them to perform academically on a much higher level than we did at the same age, to understand technology beginning practically at birth, and to socialize at a faster pace than was ever expected of us.

In developing these skills, our children are also learning others: the ability to think much more critically than we ever did at their young age, to be less complacent, *and* to challenge authority several years earlier than we did. These are not bad skills or traits. In fact, if you take a look around, you'll find that adults are achieving great success at much younger ages now than they were a generation or two ago.

However, the way your child expresses these aspects of his personality and the way you help him channel them are crucial in assisting him to grow into a productive and interested teen—and adult—who values hard work and all that it can help him achieve. In addition, your response can help him learn that challenging authority is healthy, but it is important to do so in a respectful manner that is neither dismissive nor arrogant. In addition, a thoughtful response to this question will help your child learn that sometimes he needs to comply with authority, because he is still a child, and rules are rules.

The Best Way to Respond

In case you're wondering, "Because your teacher said so," is *not* a good answer to this question! I'm not going to let you blame this one on the teachers. Rather, your response needs to do two things:

1. Open communication with your child about his frustration at having to do work he doesn't like (or finds difficult).
2. Help him understand that sometimes work that doesn't seem important or worthwhile really is beneficial.

For example, you might say a version of the following: "I know long division is difficult for you, and if you need help, we can work on it together. But it is important to learn it. Grown-ups use division all the time when they are figuring out money, and you don't always have a calculator. Also, learning how to concentrate on doing division step by step will help your brain practice concentrating really well, so that when you need to concentrate on other things that you really love, like learning a sequence of notes for a music recital, you'll be able to do it well. But even if you don't love it, you still need to work at it, because every part of school is important, and that means being respectful of school and what your teacher asks you to do."

You can apply this same concept to any complaint your child has. Explain how learning as a child will be useful when your child grows up, and also how it can be applied right now. Here's one more example: "I know that art isn't your favorite subject, but I really enjoy all the projects you bring home. Also, creating art with found objects can help you when you're a grown-up, because sometimes when you're at work and something isn't going exactly the way you wanted, you have to be very creative and figure out how to change it into something completely different so that it works differently or better. That's like 'found art'—taking one thing and changing it into something different—it's teaching your brain to be creative in a new way. The more you do that, the better you'll be at it, and it won't be so hard. But, even if you don't like it, you need to do it respectfully and work hard at it, because even when you're an adult, there are times when you have to do things you don't like, and if you don't do them well, you could get fired from your job. So I can't wait to see the best 'found art' project you've ever made!"

#8: HOW COME MY FRIENDS DON'T WANT TO PLAY WITH ME?

Angela told me her daughter Bianca (age 8) was having a really hard time socially. "Last year everything seemed fine, but now Bianca doesn't seem to be connecting with her friends in the same way," explained Angela. "She says things like, 'Mommy, why don't Lindsay, Selena, and Randi want to play with me anymore?'"

If you haven't experienced it yet, the social life of an upper-elementary-age child can become complicated— particularly (although definitely not exclusively) within the world of girls.

Uncovering the Meaning

Often beginning in third grade, although sometimes earlier or later (remember there is a range of normal), children begin developing a strong sense of real friendship. This is wonderful! It reflects your child's ability to begin understanding which other children are a good match for her own personality, strengths, and interests.

However, along with these newly developing friendships, many children experience an unexpected shift in their social lives for which they are unprepared. In some instances, your child may find herself suddenly on the outside of a social group of which she was recently just a part, or she might experience the loss of a close friend who suddenly seems more interested in other friendships. This can feel like a confusing betrayal for any child.

But what triggers such social upheaval? And why does it happen so often?

In the upper elementary grades, children's personalities and interests begin to shine through. Your child no longer wants to play with someone simply because she happens to be in the same corner of the playground or the same class—or because she is the child of your friend. She is naturally attracted to friendships with children with whom she feels most comfortable. For example, if she is athletic, she might be attracted to more sporty children; if she is a bit shy, perhaps she likes kids who are a bit on the quieter side; a private type of child might not want to be friends with one who tends to be more of a secret-sharer. Of course, there are no hard and fast rules, but your child might find her social circle changing because the children with whom she used to be friends no longer feel the same sense of connection to each other that they once did. This may be disconcerting, but it is important for her to learn how to adjust and make new friends, as long as she isn't being bullied or teased. In addition, in almost all cases, a situation is two-sided, which means that your child is *not* innocent, no matter what she tells you.

So how do you help your child through these rough patches?

The Best Way to Respond

To begin, it is helpful to understand that the feelings of social betrayal and disloyalty in elementary school seem (and are!) awful for everyone while they are happening, but in the majority of instances, they are temporary. One day, two children are enemies and next week they are, once again, friends. Keeping this perspective will help you manage your child's social upheaval in two ways. First, you will be able to reassure your child that things will soon change; and second, you will not feel nearly as devastated while your child is going through a rough social patch.

In addition, it is important to keep in mind that

since elementary (and even middle-school) friendships are typically *very* changeable, you need to ensure that *your friendships* with parents of your children's friends are not negatively impacted when the kids disagree, argue, or even seem to hate each other. While their disagreement seems to you like it will last forever, it most likely won't. In fact, while you and another parent might still be enraged with each other over a dispute between your children, the children will have long since made up.

Two of my long-time friends, and very close friends themselves, Tami and Simi experienced several years of an on-again, off-again relationship between their daughters, Sydney and Rachel (now both age 13), beginning in third grade, and continuing all through elementary school and into middle school. They realized that their friendship would only survive if they were able to separate it from their daughters' relationship with each other. They therefore developed a simple four-point creed that has taken them through their often-feuding daughters' relationship and allowed them to remain close, no matter what. Their advice will work for any parents, and I believe all parents should take Simi and Tami's advice, not only for the health of their own friendships, but for the emotional health of their children.

Tami and Simi's Creed

1. _My own child will be guilty at one time or another—she may be innocent today, but tomorrow she'll probably be guilty. It's hard to be objective about your child, but it's healthier for your child, and it makes it easier to see the other parent and child's perspective._
2. _I recognize that my child will almost always leave out the parts that make her look bad, and she will always include information that makes the other child look really awful._
3. _My child will argue with other kids 150 times (at least) before she graduates; so as long as we adults don't bring it into our relationship, we will be able to help the kids resolve their issues._
4. _Today two children can be enemies, but tomorrow they will be friends. But if we adults are still harboring anger toward each other, it will ruin our friendship—even when they are already friends again._

As you can see, the first step in helping your child is for you to become objective. This may simply mean you need to acknowledge that your child contributed to an argument, and help her take responsibility for her part in it. If this is the case, you will need to encourage her to apologize to her friend and ask that her friend acknowledge her role as well. Remember—enemies today, friends tomorrow!

If it appears that the friendship is permanently over, you will need to help your child recognize that she needs to branch out and make new friends, because the old ones (for whatever reason) no longer want to be her friend. Understandably, you will feel sad for your child. Perhaps her old friends were not especially nice about ending the friendship—but they are kids, who may not yet know how to be sensitive about such things. However, feeling sorry for her will not help her. Rather, teaching her to cope and adjust will be much more useful. Therefore, explain to her that sometimes friendships change, not because one person is good or bad, but because people become different as they get older. You will be most helpful to your child if you focus on moving forward, rather than on dwelling on the past.

Give her suggestions for how to make new friends, such as, "Talk to kids in your class, on the playground, and in your extracurricular activities and sports; join a club after school. When you meet someone you like, ask if she would like to come over to play; exchange phone numbers. Before you know it, you will have a new friend."

In less common instances, you might find that your child has consistent trouble making or keeping friends. If you find this to be the case, you may have to seek extra help or support to learn why your child has trouble socializing and to address the problem. Therefore, if your child exhibits one or more of the following behaviors, I strongly suggest that you speak to a child psychologist or other counselor specializing in the issues of children:

- avoids social interactions, shuts down, is painfully shy, or becomes anxious around children or adults
- can interact socially with adults, but kids find her annoying, clingy, or inappropriate
- has never really had friends, is often left out, teased, or bullied
- is physically aggressive, verbally abusive, mean, or angry toward other children
- is so impulsive, loud, or overly active that it annoys other children
- tells you she doesn't want or need friends, or shies away from social interaction, one-on-one or in groups
- would like to make friends, but doesn't know how to do it; despite you or teachers intervening for a year or more now, your child still can't figure out how to approach or interact with other kids in a way that they welcome
- behaves in such a way that a teacher or school administrator has recommended you seek outside help

#9: CAN YOU BUY ME COOKIES/A BOOK/POSTER BOARD? I NEED IT TOMORROW.
(OR: CAN YOU HELP ME WITH MY PROJECT? IT'S DUE IN TWO DAYS.)

Lisa, mother of Hunter (age 9), feels like she can never keep ahead of the game with her son, "I'm not sure if it is that Hunter doesn't tell me things until the last minute, or if his teacher doesn't tell him. But either way, I'm constantly running around trying to do things for him at the eleventh hour. It drives me crazy!"

There's no doubt about it, as a parent you are always doing *something* for your child or children, but is the last-minute crisis intervention a necessity, or is there a way to minimize it? In fact, is it even good for your child that you are running around bailing him out at the last minute? Let's find out.

Uncovering the Meaning

It is possible that your child's teacher has, at the very last minute, asked him to provide cookies for the class, but it is not likely. It is more plausible that your child volunteered to bring said cookies into school the next day. It is also improbable that the teacher requested poster board, clay, highlighters, a particular book, or any other supply the day before it was due.

It is much more likely—in fact, probable—that your child forgot to write down or tell you about what he needed until the last minute and is suddenly in a panic. However, if you are unsure, you can always call a few other parents in the class to check the facts. Speaking to more than one parent is necessary, because your child's best friend may also have forgotten.

If you frequently (or even sometimes) find yourself baking cupcakes at midnight or running around searching for open stores to find exactly the right supply, certainly there is a pattern that has been set up by you and your child. This is also true if you find yourself working with your child on projects or studying for tests at the last minute because he did not tell you about them in advance.

The time has come to break a pattern that is not good for either of you. It is a pattern that makes you frustrated and angry, and that is teaching your child bad habits that he will carry with him into adolescence and adulthood unless you help him change. By always bailing out your child at the last minute, you are teaching him that he doesn't need to take responsibility for his own actions, that someone will always rescue him if he doesn't do what he is supposed to do.

Is this the message you *mean* to communicate? I didn't think so!

A different response will lead to your child becoming more responsible for his behavior, and you will find yourself less likely to be jumping through last-minute hoops.

The Best Way to Respond

If your child rarely springs last-minute requests on you, it is okay to respond by saying, "I will get it for you just this once, but next time you ask for something at the last minute, I will say no and you will need to explain to your teacher why you don't have it."

However, if your child is like the many for whom waiting until the last minute is more of a pattern, your response needs to be different. Your child needs help learning that you are busy, and that you can't always rearrange your life to meet his needs. By showing him this, you introduce him to an all-important life lesson: other people's lives have value beyond satisfying his needs.

Most importantly, he must learn that there are consequences for not doing what one is supposed to do (in this case, not telling you far enough in advance that he needed something or that he had a project/test that required preparation).

In order to give your child these critical tools, your response should be a variation of the following (said *without* anger, *please*): "I'm not going to get you the poster board today. I checked with a few other parents who all told me that the teacher told you about it last week. Since you didn't tell me about it until today, you're going to have to explain that to your teacher tomorrow. Tell her we will get it tomorrow. When I see you after school tomorrow, you can tell me if you have any consequences for handing it in late. But you and I both know that if you had told me about it sooner, you would have had it on time. I'm sure next time you'll remember to tell me when you have something due."

An elementary-school-age child will benefit far more from learning this lesson than from having his supplies in on time. Even if your child has a test the next day, you can choose not to study with him at the last minute. A bad grade on one test in elementary school will have absolutely no impact on your child's academic future, but it could have a lasting, powerful, and positive impact on his decision to take greater responsibility for his actions going forward—and that will certainly have a profound effect on his academic performance as he enters middle and high school.

#10: CAN I TAKE A DAY OFF FROM SCHOOL?

Dana and Troy told me that their children Madison (age 7), Caleb (age 9), and Skylar (age 11½) frequently ask to take a day off from school. Each child has a different reason.

Troy began by explaining, "Caleb feels he knows all

the work, so he thinks he can stay home and watch TV sometimes!"

Then Dana added, "Madison wants to take a day off to stay home and spend time with me, and Skylar fakes being sick at least once every couple of months so she can try and get away with sleeping late and getting the day off."

Kids want a day off from school for all kinds of reasons. What is your child's reason? And what should you do about it?

Uncovering the Meaning

If your child asks to stay home every day, or almost as frequently, it means she is struggling with a serious issue: either one at school which is making her resistant to go, or one at home which is making her reluctant to leave. It is important to uncover this issue as soon as possible, because the longer you wait, the larger the problem will become for your child and the more difficult it will be for her to go to school each day. Some possible reasons a child might *regularly* resist going to school include the following:

- School is very difficult for the child (speak to the teacher to see if she is struggling academically and determine if further steps need to be taken to support her).
- She is having a hard time socially (being teased, bullied, or isolated). Don't assume your child will

tell you—she may be embarrassed. Ask her, and ask the teacher.

- Her home life is stressful so she doesn't want to leave each day (for example, you're in the middle of a divorce, someone is very ill, there is a great deal of fighting, there's a new baby and she's jealous).

If your child asks this question more intermittently, it is likely that she does it for one of several other reasons. For example, maybe, like Madison, she wants time alone with one parent. This is not an unreasonable request, especially in busy families when a child rarely gets to spend time alone with a parent. In this situation, I'd recommend considering whether your child's request is reasonable and valid. A planned day off together under such a circumstance might be great for both you and our child.

On each birthday I give my children a coupon for a day off from school—planned in advance—to spend with me each year. Two of my children (my daughters) use the coupons each year. We have had wonderful days off—lunch, pottery painting, manicures, shopping! My son, who started high school this year, has only used one of his coupons—about six years ago. I think he just enjoys knowing he has them. I've told him they never expire; he can take a day off from work one day in the future if he wants to, and spend it with me.

The bottom line is that while elementary school is an important time in your child's life, it is not more important than your child's emotional health or your relationship with your child. Therefore, if once in a while your child is exhausted, needs a little extra TLC, or wants some time with you, it is okay to consider letting her take a day off school, or as a compromise, go into school a couple of hours late so she can sleep late or you have breakfast with you.

The Best Way to Respond

If your child asks to stay home every day because of a psychological or academic issue, either at school or at home, it is important that you *not* give in. Avoiding dealing with the problem will only make it worse, rather than better. Instead, explain to your child that she needs to go to school and that you are going to do everything you can to make her feel better about going. Then make sure that you do so.

When your child asks you this question occasionally, you need to take into account all that we have just discussed. Don't be quick to answer no. Rather, consider the reason your child is asking, how frequently she asks, and what an occasional yes might mean to her. Also, consider my coupon idea. Giving your child one coupon a year for a day off from school will put the decision in your child's hands as to when she wants to use it. It will likely reduce how often she asks to stay home because now she must decide whether or not she should use her precious coupon.

#11: CAN I GO TO A FRIEND'S HOUSE?
(OR: CAN I HAVE A SLEEPOVER?)

Terrance's mother, Latanya, explained that Terrance (age 8) constantly asks if he can go to someone's house to play. "He knows the rule is that he needs to finish his homework before he can go anywhere, but it is still the first question he asks every day when he gets off the school bus. It drives me crazy because it seems to be the most important thing in his life, even though school-work should be!"

Most elementary-school-age children love to be social, and the older they get, the more social they become. By the upper elementary grades, it seems to be what drives them. Why is this, and how much should you let it control your child's life? Keep reading and you'll find out.

Uncovering the Meaning

As children mature into the upper elementary grades, their social needs become more complex. No longer are they satisfied playing with their friends only in school or in a group on the playground. Instead, they want to be able to deepen their friendships by spending time with other children one-on-one or in small groups.

As a general rule, this is somewhat truer for girls than it is for boys. However, older-elementary-age boys also begin asking to spend exclusive time with peers, rather than wanting only to be in large groups playing ball or running around.

In addition to wanting to form more meaningful relationships, children in the older elementary grades also begin to form friendship cliques—yes, the kind that are typically exclusive and often not especially friendly toward outside members. Although girls get the bad reputation when it comes to these cliques, they are not reserved for girls. I have seen boys left out of cliques—many of which are formed around sports prowess, knowledge of a TV show, or even an ability to play chess.

In addition to the clique, your upper-elementary-age child may also begin to explore the idea of having a "best friend" or several very close friends, either within a clique or instead of being in one. The capacity to begin bonding intimately in this way is, once again, more common with girls, but not unusual for boys. One ten-year-old girl told me that she has "bestest friends, best friends, and good friends."

Wanting to play intimately with a close friend (or small group of friends) or have a sleepover can serve many purposes. It is a way to solidify a clique, and also to affirm its exclusivity. As a parent you may not like the idea of your child being in a clique, but as long as the children in your child's clique are not hurting anyone else's feelings, bullying, teasing, being mean to, or belittling anyone, they are entitled to be friends with whomever they choose. In addition, playdates and sleepovers help create and affirm the bonds of best friends. They are a time for secrets and memories, for special codes and fabulous stories. They are not to be missed.

But what if they seem to be taking over?

The Best Way to Respond

Despite the fact that playing with friends is certainly valuable for your child's emotional development, it should have its time and place.

By all means, homework, activities, and chores should always come first. In fact if your child asks this question, relentlessly, every single day, you need to have a clear un-wavering rule that there is no socializing until absolutely everything else is done first. If your child keeps asking, you may need to change the rule so that there is no socializing at all during the week. Explain that you changed the rule because he didn't stop nagging and that you might con-sider changing it back to "no socializing until homework is done" in a couple of months if he does well this way.

In addition, it is important to set up a few guidelines for playdates and sleepovers. This will help you keep control of your child's social life. Beginning to do this now is important, because it will be harder to start when your child is a preteen or teenager. Make an effort to set these guidelines now with your child.

- "You need to ask me if you can make a plan with a friend, *not* tell me you have already arranged it. It needs to be convenient for my schedule."

- "You can only have a playdate/sleepover with a friend after I've confirmed it with his parent."
- "You can have a playdate/sleepover only at homes where I feel comfortable having you go; otherwise your friend needs to come to our house."
- "If you give me a hard time ending a playdate (whining, crying, nagging for more time), I will not let you have playdates in the future."

#12: DO I HAVE TO INVITE HER TO MY PARTY?

When Maxine and her daughter Stephanie were planning Stephanie's eleventh birthday party, Maxine became upset. "Steph wanted to exclude one girl in her class from the invitation list. I was shocked because it was so mean, and I didn't think she was like that, but Steph said this girl is mean to her and she should be able to have who she wanted at her party. I didn't let her do it though, and she was really angry with me. It wasn't one our finest moments together!"

So, at this age, how much should you get involved? What's the most important lesson your child needs to learn—independent decision-making, or something else?

Uncovering the Meaning

You might be surprised (or maybe not) to see this question in the top fifty. However, as you can see from the previous question, older-elementary-age children feel strongly about wanting to be able to control their own social lives. Choosing who to invite to a birthday party, or any other kind of party, is a big deal to them.

Like Stephanie, your child may feel justified in excluding a child. In fact she may even feel that this is the only power she has over a child who has excluded, teased, or bullied her. It is important not to discard these feelings, even though it is usually *not* right to exclude one child from an invitation list, even under these circumstances.

Your child may have other, less obvious reasons for asking this question. For example, you might find out that peers are pressuring her not to invite a particular child. They think the child is "weird," and she's afraid if she invites her they won't come to the party.

The Best Way to Respond

Typically, your response should be to tell your child that it is not right to exclude one child, even if you don't like her. Explain that, "You need to invite her, and if she doesn't like you either, she probably won't come. However, if she does, you should be as polite as you would be to any other guest."

The only exception to this is if the child has bullied your child in an extreme manner. In this case it may be in your child's best interest to respect her wishes and not extend the invitation. This will give her an opportunity to finally stand up to the bully. If you choose to make this decision, I would suggest speaking to the teacher in advance of sending the invitations so that, should the child's parent complain to anyone other than you, the school is prepared with a logical explanation.

If your child's reason for wanting to exclude one (or more than one) child isn't immediately obvious, it is worthwhile to take the time to talk to her about it, rather than assume you know the reason. This offers an opportunity for you to find out what is going on in your child's social life in a way that she may not have told you before now. Although you may not be able to give your child the quick solution she wants—since it's not usually acceptable to leave out one child—at least you will be able to open a discussion about a healthier way to resolve her bad feelings, rather than not inviting someone to her party.

3

Who's in Charge?

When your child was younger, disciplining her was probably not very complicated. She might not always have done what you said, but it is unlikely that she challenged your actual rules, or looked for loopholes through which to wiggle in order to bend and twist them. But now that she is older and becoming more independent with each passing day, it seems that discipline is a little less cut and dried.

Children in the upper elementary grades are excellent lawyers in the making. Their verbal skills, now strong and confident, are being well exercised—your child probably argues with you about all sorts of issues, but most notably about the manner in which you discipline him. As he explores his independence from you, and his greater investment in his social world, he will be much more likely to challenge not only how you discipline him, but even the very rules that you lay down. It can be an ongoing battle, leaving you depleted at the end of each day. That is, unless you learn that there are times to stand firm and times to compromise with your child.

Your child's questions will help you learn to negotiate this new territory in a way that will result in a peaceful alliance between you and your child, rather than one fraught with bickering and relentless nagging. Most importantly, in the end, you—and not your child—will still be in charge.

#13: HOW COME MY FRIENDS CAN SEE A PG-13 MOVIE/PLAY MATURE VIDEO GAMES/SIT IN THE FRONT SEAT OF THE CAR/WEAR A SHORT SKIRT/ [FILL IN THE BLANK] AND YOU WON'T LET ME?

Anabella (age 9½) and Marco (age 11½) are always saying that their parents, Valerie and Santiago, are way too strict. "Val makes most of the rules," explained Santiago, "and I support her a hundred percent because she's a great mom. We are strict because we see the craziness that is out there. But sometimes we wonder if we're going overboard, because it seems like our kids are the only ones not watching any of the TV shows or seeing any of the movies. They seem to get a lot of pressure from their friends. But they are good kids, so being strict does count for something!"

We live in a complex world, and our kids seem to grow up so fast. It can be confusing to know when to say yes and when to say no to your child, especially when peer pressure is playing a significant role. So let's try to understand the question, and by the end, you'll have a clear response for your child, even when friends are in the picture.

Uncovering the Meaning

You probably thought that your child was relatively safe from peer pressure until at least middle school, right? If you did, don't feel bad, because most parents think so too. But, actually, peer pressure begins practically as soon as your child sets foot out of the front door and into nursery school or kindergarten.

Although peer pressure has a bad reputation, it does have its merits. It teaches children the importance of behaving socially appropriately and it also shows them the value of acting cooperatively in a group situation.

However, peer pressure has not earned its bad reputation for nothing. In the upper elementary grades, children often expect to be allowed do things that in reality are too mature for their age, and also experience media (TV, movies, video games, and music) that is too sexually stimulating or violent. This expectation is caused, or at least fueled, by peer pressure. I would be remiss if I did not point out that of course the peer pressure arises in the first place because one child becomes exposed to the age-*in*appropriate experience because her own parent allows it. In other words, the buck stops with the parent—*you*!

It is easy to let your child "get away" with behaviors that are not always in her best interest. In the short run, you won't have to confront an argument, you will be the "good guy," your child will be happy, and it doesn't seem like such a big deal.

However, in the all-important long run, it is important to pick and choose carefully when you decide to relent to peer pressure. Regardless of what other parents choose to allow, a child can be emotionally damaged when she is exposed to experiences that are too emotionally mature for her developmental level. In addition, you may be unaware of some of the messages you are inadvertently sending your child.

Some examples include, but are not limited to, the following:

- Media that includes sexually inappropriate material (TV, movies, video games) can be scary and sexually stimulating for your elementary-school-age child. To drive this point home, a powerful study (found in the November 2008 issue of the journal *Pediatrics*) found that teenage girls who have a high level of exposure to TV shows with sexual content are twice as likely to become pregnant as those who watch few shows with this type of content. It is likely that the more they experience sexual media, the more "normal" it seems and the less risky. Your child may still be young, but I assure you, this media is affecting her already. Besides, you can't take media away once she becomes a teenager. And the media affect boys too—impacting on their view of girls and of the role of sexual activity in their lives.

- Scary or violent movies, TV, or even video games can cause bad dreams or fears. Once experienced, it can be difficult to get rid of them.

- Allowing your young child access to media that is above the rating recommended for her age also sends a very mixed message to your child. It is hard to expect her to obey rules if you don't. All media—TV, movies, video games—have ratings. Follow these ratings and you'll be fine. In addition, I strongly recommend you check out www.CommonSenseMedia.org and sign up for its weekly newsletter. It is the best resource I know for media-savvy parents.

- Giving in to legally prohibited behaviors before they are legal for your child (like sitting in the front seat of the car before she is old enough) can give her the message that you don't respect the law or value her safety enough. Once again, if you want your child to obey laws, now and in the future, you need to do the same.

- Regardless of whether you have a boy or a girl, giving in to clothing choices that make you uncomfortable gives your child the message that you believe fitting in with the crowd is more important than dressing in a way that is appropriate. It is fine for your child to wear clothes that you don't like (the color or style), as long as the clothing doesn't deliver a message that you don't approve of—too-short skirt/too-baggy shorts/ too-tight top/underwear sticking out of jeans, etc. This is always a fight worth having. If you don't start fighting the battles now, the war will be lost long before your child is a teen.

The Best Way to Respond

When you child asks to do something that "everyone else does," don't assume this to be fact. Begin by saying you are going to start calling all her friends to see if it is true. Many times, your child will say that you can't possibly do this, because it would embarrass her—and this will end the conversation. Similarly, you can start naming her friends one by one, asking if each child is allowed to engage in the behavior in question. Again, it is likely that at least one or two will also have "mean, strict parents" like you.

However, even if it turns out that your child is the

only one not allowed to sit in the front seat or watch the PG-13 movie, this is not a reason to give in. There will be many times in your child's life that she will be forced to confront peer pressure far greater than this, and she will have to learn to have enough inner strength to withstand it. You need to help her to do it now because it is for the right reasons.

Furthermore, learning to cope with frustration, in the form of you saying no, is one of life's greatest lessons. Your child will hear the word no many, many times in her life. If she does not know how to deal with this, she will not grow into a strong, self-sufficient adult. So, don't feel guilty, don't feel sorry for your child, and don't give in to things that you don't believe are in your child's emotional best interest. She will survive. In fact, she will flourish.

On the other hand, as your child grows up, there are times when it is fine to compromise with your child. In fact, it is a good idea to look for opportunities for compromise, especially when you have just stood firm on something big. You wouldn't want to be as flexible with a younger child, with whom you are still trying to establish rules and routines (see *The Top 50 Questions Kids Ask (Pre-K through 2nd Grade)*, Question #13), but with a child in this age-range, it will help parent effectively within the rules, while still being a little flexible. For example, if your child asks to stay up fifteen minutes later, you might say yes. If she asks if she can skip her bath one night, it could be a good time not to make a fuss about it. If she wants to play just one more game with you, go for it!

#14: IF I DO THE DISHES/CLEAN MY ROOM/SAY I'M SORRY/WRITE A LETTER/PAY YOU BACK, CAN I NOT BE PUNISHED ANYMORE?

Jordan (age 8) always tries to bargain his way out of the "bad behavior" consequence issued by his mother, Renee. Renee says that depending on the "crime," sometimes she lets him out. "The problem is that I'm not sure if he really feels sorry for what he did. He's so focused on getting out of the punishment that it seems like he's already forgotten why he got it in the first place!"

Our children can be frustrating, but at the same time, we still have to stop and marvel at their impressive new skills, including the ability to negotiate, which we sometimes take for granted.

Uncovering the Meaning

Before becoming too frustrated by your child's bargaining and unwillingness to accept a consequence (despite it being earned by poor behavior), stop and think for a minute. It is exciting to see your child beginning to develop the ability to strategize, as well as his attempt to get *you* to compromise.

Once again, you can see how he is becoming not only more sophisticated as he gets older, but feistier too. He is not simply accepting your punishment. Rather he is looking for loopholes and strategies—for ways to modify the situation. He is not telling you he expects you to remove the punishment. No, he is old enough and smart enough to know better than that. Rather, he wants to strike a deal with you—are you willing to compromise?

It is important to ask yourself whether it is in your child's best interest for you to make these types of deals. *In most cases, it is not.* By allowing your child to bargain his way out of a consequence or a punishment, you give him the message that your original punishment was meaningless. Over time, he will have less and less respect for your disciplinary techniques. He will recognize that he can always (or almost always) bargain his way down from the original, stricter consequence into a compromise of his own creation. By the time he reaches high school (or even before), he will engage in a negative behavior, already having calculated this "formula for the consequence" in advance of "committing the crime." Effectively, you will have lost complete control over disciplining your child.

In addition, allowing bargaining and compromise after you issue a fair punishment teaches your child that bargaining and compromise are always options when you do something wrong. This is simply not the case. There will be many times in your child's life when he hurts someone's feelings, or does something wrong in school or at a job, and there will be no compromise as to how he is treated—the friendship will be lost, he will have failed the class, or he will be fired from the job.

Your child needs to learn to face his own bad behavior, the failure with which it is associated, and the consequences it produces. You need to help him achieve this now on a small level, so he is prepared to cope with it later on when it is harder to manage emotionally.

The Best Way to Respond

When your child asks if he can do something to take away his punishment, your response needs to be a variation of the following: "I picked this consequence because it fits your behavior. You will need to stick with the consequence until it is finished. I know you are not happy about it, but that's the way it is. There is nothing you can do to change this. We are not making any deals or striking any bargains. That's that." Don't be surprised if your child gets angry or upset the first time or two you say this, especially if he is used to you compromising in the past. But don't worry, he'll get used to it, and it will make him a *much* stronger person.

#15: WHY DO I HAVE TO CLEAN MY ROOM IF I LIKE IT MESSY?
(OR: WHY DO I NEED TO GO TO BED IF I'M NOT TIRED?)

Despite the fact that Curtis likes things neat and tidy, his daughter Amber (age 10) has him stumped with this question. "I'm not sure whether I should make her tidy her room or if I should let her keep it messy. I don't want to inflict my way of doing things on her, if it's really not what she likes. I'm really conflicted."

Like many parents, Curtis isn't always sure where to draw the line when it comes to allowing his child to express her personality, independent thoughts, and decision-making ability. However, once you understand this question and how to respond to it the right way, you will find that answering it will be much easier.

Uncovering the Meaning

When your child asks you this or any similar "why… if…" question, resist the urge to believe that she is simply being combative. Rather, you will experience the behavior as a little less frustrating if you recognize that she is beginning to practice learning how to separate from you. For many children, this starts in the late elementary years, particularly if your child has one or more older siblings propelling her to grow up even faster. Arguing the opposite of what you want (you like it neat—she wants it messy; you want her to go to sleep—she is suddenly not tired; you want her to eat dinner—she's not hungry), gives her some practice defining her own space and forming her own opinion, even if she is not really all that sure of herself yet.

This brings us to the next issue—should you allow your child to make these decisions, to express herself in this way? Or should you insist that she do it your way? The best answer to this is yes—and yes.

By asking you this question, your child is letting you know that she wants some recognition as an independent-thinking person, and you can give this to her in ways we will discuss in a minute.

However, your child is not old enough to know what time she should go to sleep, whether or not her clothes should be picked up off her bedroom floor, or what time dinner is served (if she is really not hungry, perhaps she's been eating too much junk food before dinner). An elementary-age child may want to feel independent, but it is *not* in her best interest actually to be independent. In fact, if you allow your child to flex these fledgling muscles of independence too much, it will be scary for her. She requires clear boundaries, limits, and a strong sense of the rules and regulations in your family. Developmentally, she will respond to this very, very well, even if she complains about it.

The Best Way to Respond

A clear response to this question should be similar to the following: "You need to clean your room because that is the rule of the house. I know you don't want to do it and that right now you like it messy. But the rule is that it needs to be tidied up. We can compromise a little. You can keep one corner a little messy, but the rest really needs to be cleaned up."

The areas in which you can and *should* allow your child to express independence include:

- choosing which clothing she wants to wear (from an appropriate selection)
- choosing her own friends (you should not require your child to be friends with your friends' children anymore; see Chapter Two, Question #12, for more about this)
- choosing her own extracurricular activities (but *not* overscheduling herself)
- involving her in the selection of weekend activities that your family chooses
- allowing her room to be a little messier than you would choose, especially if you are a neat freak by all objective accounts other than your own
- allowing her to participate in the selection of meals cooked and served in your family on a weekly basis. She should not be forced to eat food that you know she consistently does not like. She should still be required to try new foods. Beginning in elementary school, some kids love to help with the cooking

and become quite good at it—it gives them a great
feeling of independence.

#16: DO I HAVE TO?

Julie, mother of Logan (age 8½), braces herself for whining
every time she asks her son to do anything she thinks he
won't want to do. She explains, "Whether I ask him to pick
up his toys, take a bath, brush his teeth, do his homework,
bring in the groceries, be nice to his sister, go to sleep, wake
up—you name it—it's his favorite response. It drives me
crazy. 'Yes, you have to,' I always say. 'I wouldn't be asking
you to do it, if I didn't want you to!' It doesn't make a difference though; he still continues to ask that question."

I have to agree with Julie—this is an annoying question. So what is the best way to manage it? Keep reading
to find out.

Uncovering the Meaning

"Do I have to?" is actually a rhetorical question. In fact,
if you think of it more like a statement than a question,
you will find yourself less frustrated by it. Your child
doesn't really expect you to change your mind and tell
him that he doesn't have to do what you asked him to
do. Rather, the question is his way of expressing his
dislike for having to do it.

However, what I find especially interesting is that,

despite the fact that most children don't expect their parents to change their minds, many will not follow through with a task after asking this question, unless they receive clear, affirmative responses from their parents—despite having been told to complete the task the first time. Here is an example of a typical scenario:

Mom: "Tyler, please pick up the dirty laundry from your floor." (Mom walks out.)

Tyler (age 9), screaming after her: "Do I haaaaave to?" (Mom doesn't hear.)

Later that day…

Mom: "Tyler, you haven't tidied up your room like I asked you!"

Tyler: "But Mom, when I asked you if I *had* to, you didn't answer, so I didn't think I *really* had to do it."

Mom: "Tyler, you knew you were supposed to clean up."

Tyler: "But Mom, when I asked if I had to, you didn't say yes."

Mom: "Oh boy!"

If this or a similar scenario seems familiar to you, you're not alone! Older-elementary-age children are beginning to learn how to be manipulative in many different ways to get around your discipline. It is important for you to learn these so that you can maintain the upper hand with your child and not lose control of the discipline. The technique that Tyler employed is fairly sneaky and smart, and it actually has a handy psychological name that can be applied to many different types of situations. It's called *passive-aggressive* behavior and here's an explanation of how it works.

When someone is angry, he can choose to express his anger in one of several different ways. He might yell, scream, or break things—this is considered an aggressive response. He might tell someone verbally that he is angry and try to problem-solve the situation—this would be considered a healthy response. Or he might express his anger by passively, sometimes subconsciously, refusing to do what he is supposed to do, all the time blaming the fact that he is not doing it on someone or something else—often the person with whom he is angry. This is passive-aggressive behavior.

You may see your child behaving like this at other times. For example, if he is angry with you for making him go to sleep early as a punishment, he may respond passive-aggressively by telling you that he doesn't like the dinner you cooked; a jealous child may passive-aggressively ruin a sibling's birthday party by deliberately having a toileting accident during the party.

Children who behave in this manner need both discipline and sympathy. In the case of this question, you cannot allow your child to get away with not accomplishing a task simply because you did not respond affirmatively to the question. He needs to know that your first request stands, no matter what is said afterwards. This type of passive-aggressive behavior is unacceptable.

You may need to seek professional assistance if your

child behaves in a more complex (perhaps less conscious) passive-aggressive way (like having toileting accidents). A child psychologist or other qualified child therapist can help you assess whether your child needs help to manage underlying psychological issues that could be causing him emotional distress.

If you don't address your child's fledgling passive-aggressive behaviors now, there is a much greater chance that, as he grows up, these will become part of his general way of coping with and avoiding uncomfortable emotional situations.

People do not enjoy interacting with other adults who engage in passive-aggressive behaviors. Examples of adult passive-aggressive behaviors include:

- acting in an annoying way toward someone with whom one is angry
- sulking
- promising to do something and then deliberately not following through
- saying something hurtful and pretending one didn't realize that it would upset the person
- "forgetting" to do something that one promised to do
- never expressing anger in a healthy, productive way

Therefore, the way you respond to this question should be with the goal of helping your child recognize that any negative behavior beyond the rhetorical question is not acceptable.

The Best Way to Respond

When your child asks you this question (and, unlike Tyler's mom, you do hear it!), your response should include a variation of the following: "When I ask you to do something, it is because I want you to do it. Responding with 'Do I have to?' makes me angry, but it doesn't make me change my mind. So, yes, you still have to do it. Also, I would like it if you would *not* ask me that question next time I ask you to do something."

If your child makes a habit of asking you this question, you can institute a consequence; for example, "I've asked you several times not to ask me that question every time I ask you to do something. It is disrespectful because it makes me feel that you don't believe that I meant it the first time I asked. From now on, when you ask me that question, I'm going to give you an extra chore to do—just so you know how much I mean it when I ask you to do something." Then, don't forget to follow through with your consequence.

Next, if you find that your child is using this question in a passive-aggressive way to try to get out of fulfilling tasks that you have assigned, you need to clearly address the issue: "You need to do what I ask you to do whether or not I respond to your question about whether you 'have to.' Once I've asked you to do something, it means you have to do it, even if you don't want to or if you're angry with me about it. It is sneaky and manipulative to try and get out of something by pretending that you thought you didn't have to do it because I didn't answer that question—especially if I didn't even hear you asking me. Sneaky behavior gets a negative consequence." Then issue a consequence. Your lesson will be taught, and hopefully you will quickly break your child of passive-aggressive behavior.

#17: HOW COME YOU CAN HAVE DIET SODA/COFFEE AND I CAN'T?

Traci and Derek's children Leigh (age 12), Spencer (age 10½), and Reilly (age 9) are relentless in their pursuit of "fair" treatment. They believe they should be allowed to drink diet soda, especially since their parents do so. Derek explained, "I don't think it's healthy for the kids to drink diet soda, and I also feel that it is hypocritical to say no to them if one of us is drinking it." Traci doesn't completely agree with her husband. "I agree that it's not great for their health, but I don't think there is anything wrong with having different rules for adults and children. Why should I have to give up diet soda?"

What do you think?

Uncovering the Meaning

When your child asks this question—about diet soda, coffee, R-rated movies, staying up late, or anything else that *you* are "allowed" to do or have, but you don't permit your child to do or have—it represents yet another way she is trying to push the limits of your discipline.

At the same time, your child is legitimately trying to determine her behavioral and emotional boundaries as she grows up. It is up to you to clearly delineate these boundaries between adult and child, and even between older and younger siblings. This will result in the greatest possibility of reducing and even eliminating the chance that your child will be confused about where she stands, which could result in her behaving in ways that are too sophisticated, difficult to manage, rude toward you and other adults, and far more empowered as a child than is appropriate.

It is therefore perfectly appropriate and acceptable for you—the adult—to engage in behaviors that you do not allow your child to experience because she is too young.

The Best Way to Respond

The best way to respond to this question is to make it clear that, as an adult, there are many things you can and will do and that you may not permit your child to do. Your response might sound similar to the following: "I get to drink coffee because I'm a grown-up and coffee is a grown-up drink. One day when you're much older, you'll get to drink it too. Coffee has caffeine in it, which isn't healthy for children's growing brains, but is perfectly safe for adults if you only drink a couple of cups a day like I do. There are many things that adults get to do that kids can't. But there are also lots of things that you can do now that you couldn't do when you were younger, or that your younger sister can't do. As you get older, you will get to do even more things. That's the way it works. You'll have to trust me to make the right decisions for you, and I won't change my mind just because you don't agree with the decision."

When it comes to diet soda, you may have to be prepared to explain to your child why it is healthy for you to drink diet soda, but it is not healthy for her. After all, the chemicals are no healthier for you than they are for her! However, one legitimate argument is that her brain is still developing while yours has finished doing so. As the parent, you have the prerogative to make decisions that are in the best interest of your child—regardless of whether you make these same choices for yourself.

Remember, being a parent is not about being fair in your child's eyes, or about being your child's friend. It is about making sure she is emotionally and physically healthy, now and for as long as you can leverage these types of choices for her.

#18: WHY CAN'T YOU JUST LEAVE ME ALONE?

Regina says she is tired of her son Brendan (age 8) who, in her opinion, seems to be behaving like a teenager before he is even a preteen. "Brendan is constantly telling me to leave him alone," explains Regina. "I thought that wouldn't happen until he was much older. Whenever he gets upset or angry, those are his first words, and then he often stomps off to his room. Sometimes I let him go, because I figure if he's so upset, I should let him cool down. But other times I don't because I think it's really rude. I'd like him to learn a better way to handle his feelings."

Regina may not realize it, but this is a common, albeit annoying, question asked by many children who are upset or frustrated when they don't get their way. The *real* question is what is the best way for you to respond to it?

Uncovering the Meaning

When a child is confronted with a situation he finds very frustrating, upsetting, or annoying, there are a couple of different ways he might respond. A child who has successfully developed the ability to express his feelings will tell you how he feels, even if he is angry with you or upset with the situation. He might cry or yell a bit, but he will be able to express his feeling appropriately.

However, a child who has not yet learned the skill of frustration tolerance (which means he becomes frustrated or angry very easily when faced with a situation that upsets, angers, or frustrates him) might respond in one of two ways. He might *act out* (lose his temper, cry, yell, blame others, and, in an extreme situation, physically hurt someone). *Or* he might *escape* (leave the situation completely, have difficulty hearing feedback that might be negative, or refuse to participate any more in an activity). When a child has poor frustration tolerance, he will often ask the question, "Why can't you just leave me alone?" Either he will yell the question as part of an acting-out temper tantrum, or he will ask it as he is leaving, as part of an attempt to escape a situation with which he doesn't want to cope.

In either scenario, it is not in your child's best interest to allow this behavior to continue. To begin, it is rude and disrespectful to you. In addition to that, *it is essential that your child learns to effectively confront and cope with frustration.* If you allow him to run away from tough situations by giving in to his demand to be left alone, you will not teach him this critical life skill. He will not keep friends by telling them to leave him alone when they argue. He will not be able to demand that teachers leave him alone when he is frustrated or upset, particularly in the upper grades—they will think he is immature. He won't be able to tell his boss one day to leave him alone when he's angry—he'll be fired! Now is the time to teach your child this skill and to correct this behavior. It will get *much* harder as he gets older.

The Best Way to Respond

The next time your child asks—or demands—that you leave him alone, your response should communicate that it is not acceptable for him to speak to you disrespectfully.

He needs to know that you will only entertain the possibility of him being left alone if he asks politely and calmly, and that first you and he need to discuss why he wants to be left alone and then decide whether that is the best choice for that time. For example, your response may sound something like the following: "I am not going to answer that question, because it is disrespectful for you to be screaming at me to be left alone simply because you don't like the fact that I have taken away the computer and TV. You didn't listen when I asked you to turn it off and this is the consequence. You don't get to be left alone for that. First, you need to calm down and we can discuss it. You don't get the electronics back and you don't get to be left alone by being rude. Now, what can I do to help you calm down?"

Here is another example—of course, these are just to give you an idea of what to say; your situation and your child may require a slightly different approach: "First, you need to turn around and come back here right now. It is rude to leave in the middle of a conversation. You may not be happy that you lost the game that we were playing, but that is not a reason to leave. It is also not okay for you to yell that you want me to leave you alone. That is disrespectful and if you do it again, there will be a consequence."

4

"I'm Scared"

As children enter the older elementary years, the fears of earlier childhood—separation, the dark, the doctor—typically fade. That being said, if your child is at the younger end of this age range, you should take a look at *The Top 50 Questions Kids Ask (Pre-K through 2nd Grade)*. As I have explained, children's behavior is always on a continuum—some older kids may still be asking questions in the younger categories and vice versa. This is perfectly normal.

In general though, as children become true "big kids," inching their way closer and closer to being tweens, they begin taking a much more critical look at the world around them, seeing it with all its imperfections (this includes their parents' flaws). Their fears reflect a feeling that not all is right with the world, and the fear-driven questions that your child asks will clearly illustrate this.

Of course, as I offer you insights toward becoming more psychologically minded, it is always important to know when your child's fears—and the questions they generate—might not be within the healthy, normal range. The guidelines below give you a good idea of when you may want to speak to a school counselor, your child's doctor, a child psychologist, or other therapist specializing in children:

- your child's fear is interfering with her ability to function in daily life partially or fully (for example, but not limited to, they prevent her from falling asleep or they wake her up during the night, she is so distracted by them that her schoolwork or social life is suffering)
- his fear has lasted for more than a couple of weeks, and no matter what you say or do, it has not remitted even a little and may be getting worse
- the fear was not precipitated by anything you can pinpoint, or if it was, the fear has outlived the precipitant by more than a couple of weeks
- your child's fear is causing stress for the whole family because it limits everyone's choices, behavior, and actions
- you have a "gut feeling" that, compared to the fears of other kids, your child's fear is not healthy

NOTE: I believe that parents should follow their gut feelings in almost all situations. After all, who knows your child better than you? So don't ignore your instincts. I have experienced many situations in which parents have come to see me after being dismissed by doctors, teachers, counselors, and even family members who didn't think there was anything wrong with their children. However, the parents knew something wasn't quite right. In many of these situations, by respecting the parents' gut feelings, and investigating further, I have found that the parents were correct, and I was able to diagnose learning or emotional difficulties that certainly needed to be addressed.

Now that you have an understanding about the developmental issues surrounding children's fears, let's get to the questions.

#19: ARE YOU GETTING A DIVORCE?

You might be surprised to learn that this was one of the most common fear-related questions submitted by parents of children in this age group.

Children worry about divorce and ask the question when their parents argue, regardless of whether there is any indication that their parents might be getting divorced. They also ask it when they have overheard conversations that may lead them to believe (whether or not it is true) that their parents may be separating or divorcing. Despite the fact that divorce is so commonplace in the world today, it is still a significant fear of most children and teens. The comments from these parents reveal this fear:

- "Every time one of us even raises our voice to one another in anger, our oldest child, Erica (age 9), asks if we are getting divorced. It's almost comical. But it does distract us from our argument. Perhaps that's her plan!"
- "The morning after Craig (age 10) overhears us fighting in our room at night—of course we thought he was asleep—he asks if we're getting divorced."
- "I have to be careful when I gossip to my mom on the phone because if Tyrone (age 7) or Lacey (age 11) hear anything, they think I'm talking about their dad and me, and they think we're getting divorced."

Uncovering the Meaning

When a child asks this question often, it is usually an indication that his parents are arguing or fighting too frequently and too intensely in front of their child—regardless of whether divorce is actually in the cards. Sometimes in the midst of an argument, one partner will threaten to leave or will do so temporarily. This can understandably also trigger a child's fear of divorce.

Clearly, in this type of scenario, the adults' behavior is triggering the child's question.

It is important for you to reflect on your family situation and determine whether your child's question about divorce is being triggered by too much fighting among the adults. Living like this is stressful for a child, making it difficult to sleep or to focus on school and homework. Children in high-stress homes, filled with fighting and yelling, are less likely to want friends to come over and are more likely to be anxious, depressed, or sad, as well as angry themselves— after all, anger is being role-modeled for them.

When a child asks this question directly after witnessing an argument, in a home where arguing is not the norm, it is more likely that the child is worried because he is not accustomed to his parents fighting and fears that this may mean they are getting divorced.

Last, when a child accidentally overhears discussion of real divorce—yours or someone else's—it is understandable that he will want to address his fear and clarify what he heard by asking the question.

The Best Way to Respond

If you are *absolutely confident* that you are not getting divorced, you should tell your child this using a variation of the following: "Grown-ups have arguments just like kids. Sometimes they can be loud and sound scary to you. But even when we have huge arguments, we still love each other, and we are not getting divorced."

If you believe that you argue too frequently in your home, you should consider adding the following (and really mean it): "We are going to work really hard at fighting less often, especially in front of you, because we can see how stressful it is for you."

If you find that, despite trying, you are not able to reduce your arguing, I suggest that you seek marital therapy with a psychologist or other counselor *highly experienced* in providing couples therapy. You would be surprised at how well it can work to receive help from a third party, expertly trained for just this purpose.

If your child overhears you having a discussion about someone else's divorce and thinks it was about you, it is important to clarify that you were not talking about your family. Respecting the other family's privacy is important, though. Only tell your child if the family has given you permission to do so.

However, if your child overhears you discussing your own divorce before you were ready to tell your child, you cannot lie. Ideally, it is best for both parents to answer this question together, whenever possible. Be truthful and simple in your response. You may not have everything worked out yet because you had not been planning on telling him yet, but a child this age needs an answer containing the following elements:

- Explain that although you don't love each other anymore, you both still love him very much and will continue to take care of him together as you have always done (to the extent that this is true, of course).

- Be clear that it is not anyone's fault that you are divorcing—especially not his. Sometimes grown-ups fall out of love, or they have lots of arguments and don't get along anymore, kind of like kids who don't stay friends forever.
- Explain what the new living arrangements will be and how visitation will work. If it is not worked out yet, do the best you can, and explain that it will change.
- Give him a time line—to the best of your ability—for when his life will change.

#20: IS THE PLANE GOING TO FALL?
(OR: WHAT HAPPENS IF THE ENGINE CATCHES FIRE? WHAT WOULD HAPPEN IF A WING FELL OFF?)

Michelle and Brian enjoy traveling with their children. However, their daughter Briana (age 8) becomes terribly anxious every time the trip involves flying. "She will begin to ask if we're going to crash, if the plane is going to break, and if it's going to fall, weeks before the trip. By the time we're ready to leave, she's in a panic!"

In this post-9/11 world, it doesn't seem surprising that children are worried about flying (or, should I say, crashing). But in reality, kids were afraid of it long before that. Let's face it, even many adults are afraid of flying and have been since planes were invented.

Uncovering the Meaning

Your child's fear has a lot to do with being out of control. There is nothing you can personally do to prevent the plane you are in from crashing, and most of us don't know the first thing about flying, so we don't even know whether the pilot's doing a good job or not. We don't even get to meet the pilot, except via the announcement system. The more out-of-control a person—child or adult—feels, the more stressed and nervous she becomes about her safety. What's more, the fear can become even greater for children because they know and understand even less about what is going on than do the adults.

Jodi, a mom I met, told me, "If the pilot sounds organized and businesslike, I feel calm, but if he sounds too friendly and chatty, I get worried that he's going to be distracted and flaky. My husband likes chatty pilots because the information they give makes him feel more relaxed. Go figure!" Clearly, there is nothing rational in either of their feelings, but each is trying to wrangle a perception of control from the sound of the pilot's voice in order to feel comforted.

One important question to ask yourself is whether you are transferring any of your anxiety about flying to your child. Kids notice their parents' body language, mannerisms, and levels of stress, as well as overt language. If you are worried about flying, it is very likely that you will inadvertently communicate this concern to your child.

The *real* truth is that flying is actually safer than driving in a car. The statistics show us that you are more than five hundred times as likely to die in a car accident as in the air. In fact, between October and December of 2001, there were one thousand more highway fatalities than in the same period the year before, because after 9/11 so many people believed they would be safer driving than flying that there were simply more cars on the roads.

It is important to not give in to your child's fear of flying, because she will find it much more difficult to master this fear at an older age. You also don't want to let it control your family's lifestyle. Therefore, now that you understand how safe it is to fly, you are ready to answer your child's question with confidence.

The Best Way to Respond

Although this is not a situation in which there are any guarantees, I very strongly recommend you respond to this question by saying as clearly and forcefully as possible: "No, the plane is *not* going to fall." If the very unlikely occurs—your plane crashes—and happily you survive, it is true that your child may confront you with the fact that you were not completely truthful. However,

I am confident that this will not be top-most on your list of concerns, having just survived a plane crash! If this happens to you, please email me at DrSusan@ DrSusanBartell.com, and I will give you personal support for managing this unique situation.

For every other time you fly, it is important to instill a sense of security and safety in your child. If she asks you specifics ("What happens if the engine catches on fire or a wing falls off?"), say the following and repeat variations of it as many times as necessary: "Planes are made with very, very strong material. They fly all the time and get checked every time they fly. They also have many backup systems that get checked every time. Even if there were to be an emergency, the pilots are trained to handle it. Planes hardly ever have accidents or problems; in fact, they have them much, much less often than cars, and you go in a car, every day! We are safe. I would never take you on a plane if I didn't think you would be safe."

#21: WHO WILL TAKE CARE OF ME IF YOU DIE?

"When Johnny (age 11) asked me this question, it really took me by surprise," explained his dad, John Sr. "I didn't even realize he worried about such heavy things, and to be honest—rightly or wrongly—we hadn't even thought about it seriously until he brought it up."

Like John, many parents are surprised by this question—and are often unprepared with an adequate response. We find it painful to think about our own mortality, but luckily for us, our kids are sometimes a bit more practical.

Uncovering the Meaning

Preschool- and early-elementary-age kids usually worry about death in a more "bodily" sense. If you have read *The Top 50 Questions Kids Ask (Pre-K through 2nd Grade)*, you'll see that the top question about death in this age group is, "Does it hurt when someone dies?" Now, in the older elementary years, a child's fears are more sophisticated and perhaps more pragmatic.

As I have promised you, throughout this book I will offer you as many psychological insights as possible into child development. Here is another one: Children in this age group are rapidly moving out of the world of fantasy and make-believe, and into a developmental phase that reflects greater interest in the concrete, black and white facts of the real world. Therefore the fact that they are pragmatic—even when fearful—makes sense. Children in this stage love rules and are concerned with right and wrong, fair and unfair. They want to know exactly what to expect at all times. We will continue to discuss this throughout the chapter as we explore other questions. But for now, it's important to know that your child is asking this question not only because he is fearful of you dying, but because he really does want to know that there is a plan that will be executed should you die. And guess what? He's not wrong to expect this or to be privy to the information. Therefore, your answer can't be, "Don't worry, I've taken care of it."

The Best Way to Respond

If you do have a plan, you should share it with your child. If it includes more than one person or a succession of people, make sure you explain the plan fully. If your child is in frequent contact with the potential guardian, it's a good idea to let this person know about your conversation with your child. This is because your child may bring it up, and the adult should be prepared to talk to your child about it reassuringly, if necessary, in a way that is consistent with what you explained.

I have known of situations when a child has been unhappy with his parents' choice of guardians. Of course the chances of both parents dying (or otherwise being removed from his life) are unlikely. However it is *not* impossible. Your now practical child realizes this and does not want to have to risk spending many years with someone he doesn't like. The thought of this can cause anxiety for a child, and you cannot always assume you know why a child doesn't like your choice, so it's important to ask. In many cases, a child's concern is misplaced and can be alleviated. For example, he may have heard an aunt yell at her children once or twice and be worried that she would be mean to him. When you remind him that you yell sometimes too—that all parents do—he will be calmer.

But what if his rationale for not liking your choice is legitimate—the aunt really is mean to her kids, but she is your closest relative? In some cases it is worth considering a change. Sometimes a very close friend is a better choice than an unpleasant relative (as long as the friend agrees, of course). You will need to make sure you have a clearly constructed, legally airtight will, in the event that it would have to be enforced. But if it means that your child would be psychologically better off, it is worth it.

If you can't answer this question, when your child asks it, it is time to make a plan. Tell your child the following: "That is an excellent question, and since we haven't figured it out yet, we need to do so right away. It's a big decision. The adults will discuss it, and we will let you know as soon as we decide—probably in the next couple of weeks."

This is not a decision for which you should solicit your child's opinion. You and your child may not agree as to who would be the best guardian for him. He may not know who would manage the finances most efficiently, who would be the most consistent parent-figure, and who would actually agree to do it if asked. You need to follow through on making your short list, narrowing it down, and approaching your candidate right away. As soon as the person has agreed, tell your child. Then make a legal will immediately. This is one of the most important and responsible decisions you will execute as a parent. *Without this, your child could become a ward of the state overnight.*

#22: WOULD YOU BE MAD AT ME IF...?

As we have begun to discuss in the previous section, older-elementary-age kids love rules and are very worried about what is right and what is wrong. It is for this reason that your child may so often check to see if you would be angry with her for doing something that is considered breaking the rules.

My daughter Mollie (age 11) will frequently watch a child on a TV sitcom or reality show who is behaving badly (having a tantrum, being rude, acting mean) and then turn to me and say "What would *you* do if *we* behaved like that?" I always respond to her by saying the following: "I would be angry if you behaved like that because it is bratty/mean/rude behavior. I might even have to punish you. But since I *know* you aren't planning to behave like that, I don't think I have to worry about it, right?" Mollie will laugh and agree. Sometimes she asks me what the punishment would be, and I tell her. However, Mollie is typically a very well-behaved child and a worrier, so in her case I downplay the possibility of consequences because they are very rarely necessary for her.

Uncovering the Meaning

Mollie and other children in this age range want to be very clear about exactly what their parents' expectations are for them. Most of the time your child will be afraid to disappoint you. Sometimes she won't mind disappointing or angering you, but she still wants to be clear what the consequences will be so she can determine whether she is willing to test a particular boundary.

For these reasons, you need to be explicit about your expectations. Creating structure is important beginning from the time your child can walk and talk, but it is no more important than now, when your child's entire personality is developmentally rule-governed. If your home doesn't yet function in an orderly, rule-driven manner, it is time to start. This doesn't mean a police state! But a few simple rules are critical to help your child feel secure and internally organized, which translates into a feeling of emotional safety:

- Create a regular after-dinner-to-bedtime routine that basically doesn't change.
- Develop a regular school-morning routine that gets your child to school on time every day.
- Ensure that homework and after-school activities and sports are always a priority (before play, TV, video, and computers).
- Remember that positive reinforcement for good behavior comes before punishment for bad.
- Don't threaten if you can't/won't follow through.

- By this age cheating, lying, stealing, hitting, kicking, punching, and spitting are not to be accepted with forgiveness, or your child will not learn to stop doing them. The consequence for these should differ depending on your child's age and how many times a behavior has occurred. If the behaviors continue or get worse (particularly physical behaviors), you may want to consider speaking to your child's doctor, a school counselor, or a child psychologist or other therapist specializing in kids.

The Best Way to Respond

Keeping in mind that your child is trying to understand the rules, it is best to respond to this question as clearly as possible—even if you are asked it a hundred times a day. Since kids this age are so concrete and factual, yours may not generalize from one example to the next. Just because you respond yes today to the question, "Would you be mad if I eat on the couch in the den?" it doesn't mean she won't ask you tomorrow if you would be mad if she ate on the carpet in the den.

Your response should include whether or not such a behavior would make you angry, why it would (or wouldn't upset you), and, if necessary, what the consequence might be. You can use my response (on page 86) to Mollie as a template for how to respond to many different questions.

For example, in response to the question about eating on the couch you might say, "Yes, I would be mad. First, you know that we have a rule about eating only in the kitchen. Second, I would not be happy if anything spilled on the couch. If I find that you have been eating on the couch, you will not be allowed to watch TV for three days—in any room of the house."

#23: ARE YOU GOING TO GET A TICKET?
(OR: ARE YOU DRIVING TOO FAST?)

By now I bet you know exactly what I'm going to say—and you would be right. The reason your child may ask this question so often and probably seems concerned about traffic safety in general is because of her general interest in rules—and making sure that you're following them.

Following rules is why kids love board games so much—they are all about rules. It's also why your child might get furious when someone else cheats or breaks the rules. "My girls panic when they see a police car," explains Natalie, mother of Paige (age 9) and Elizabeth (age 8). "Their first questions are always, 'Are you speeding? Are you going to get a ticket?' I always have to tell them to calm down; I'm not speeding."

Uncovering the Meaning

Just as your child is worried about following rules herself, she is equally concerned that you are following rules. Aside from the rules of the road, children in this age range are aghast and terrified at the thought of sneaking into a second movie without paying, expressing dissatisfaction with service in a store or restaurant, or even taste-testing a new flavor of ice cream when they know in advance that they are not going to buy it. Appreciate this innocence now, because by adolescence it might be long gone!

However, the rules of the road are by far the most predominant concern for children this age. The sudden presence of a police car is likely to cause you to react by slowing down, muttering, or otherwise inadvertently cuing your child that you are tense. The message is clear: the presence of a police officer is a big neon-flashing sign to "follow the rules," not only for children, but for adults as well.

But when you behave like this, your child becomes worried that you are going to get into trouble—either because you haven't been following the rules, or because she fears that, in the adult world, you can get in trouble even when you do follow the rules. Remember, learning about rules is still somewhat uncharted territory for your child, and you will have to help to reduce her fears—particularly about the law. It's important for her to see police and other law enforcement officers as a positive, rather than negative, part of her life so that, should she ever need help, she is not afraid to ask for it.

Of course, you also need to ask yourself, are you driving too fast? Perhaps your child is scared, and rather than being confident enough to tell you directly, she is trying to let you know in this way. Self-reflection is important—for your child's physical *and* emotional safety.

The Best Way to Respond

Sometimes it is best to respond to a child's question with a question. This will help you figure out what your child is really worried about. This is one of those times. Ask her the following question: "What's making you think I might get a ticket?" (Or "What's making you think that I'm driving too fast?") Listen carefully to your child's response to this question, asking others if you need to. If your child has noticed that you get panicky whenever you pass a police car, respond by saying, "Sometimes when I see a police car, I slow down just to make sure that I'm not speeding. But I am a careful driver, and people don't get tickets for no reason. Police officers have special machines that monitor how fast people drive so they don't pull you over by mistake."

If your child indicates that she thinks you are speeding, explain that you keep an eye on the speedometer to make sure you are within the speed limit. Suggest that she can also watch the traffic to see that most people travel around the same speed.

However, if you really are speeding, thank her for noticing, and tell her that you will begin to watch the speedometer more carefully from now on.

#24: WHAT WOULD HAPPEN IF YOU LOST YOUR JOB?

When Camilla came home from work one night, her son Thomas (age 8) asked her this question. Since she had never expressed any concern about losing her job, she wasn't sure why he was asking. "Why are you wondering that?" she asked Thomas. He replied, "Well, Ryan told us that his dad lost his job yesterday, and now they have to live with Ryan's grandma. So what would happen if *you* lost your job?"

This is a common question, asked by many kids, even when their parents' jobs are completely stable. As you can see, it might be triggered by hearing about another child's parent losing his job. As with so many of the fears during this stage, this question reflects your child's knowledge that life may not always go as planned. However, given his need for rules, he also wants to know that when something goes wrong, there will be a plan for how to handle it.

Uncovering the Meaning

This question is similar to, "Who will take care of me if you die?" Your child is asking it because, should this serious event occur, he wants to know that you—the adult—have formulated a plan to manage it.

Although it is not necessary or even advisable for you to give your child a comprehensive description of your plan should you lose your job, it is important that you offer him direct, clear information that indicates that you don't plan to just "wing it" should you be unfortunate enough to lose your job.

Your child is less likely to ask you this question if you are self-employed, because at this age most kids believe that self-employment protects one from the perils of unemployment. However, some kids are a bit more perceptive or have already experienced a family member losing a business, so they know better. If this is the case, your child may ask you, so you should be prepared.

The Best Way to Respond

If your employment is secure, your response should sound something like this: "It is very, very unlikely that I will lose my job. I have been working there for a long time, and there is absolutely no reason that it should happen. However, if I ever think it might, I will start looking for another job in advance. If I was to suddenly lose my job, I will immediately start looking for another job and find one as soon as possible. While I look, we might have to cut back on vacations, eating out, and extra treats (or realistically whatever you will have to do), but we will be fine. Taking care of you is my top priority, so don't worry!"

On the other hand, we do live in an unstable economic climate, so it is possible that your position is not secure. Perhaps your child's question was even prompted by adult conversation he overheard concerning the economy or your job. If this is your situation, it is not fair to reassure your child of a sense of security that may be somewhat false. However, it is not beneficial to alarm your child. Therefore, your response should be similar to the following one: "Sometimes adults don't stay in jobs forever because companies hire too many people and then have to let some go (or because they stop making enough money and they can't afford to pay everyone). That is happening where I work. So right now I'm looking for a new job. I'm going to keep looking until I find one. I may end up staying at my job, but I may end up changing to a new one. If I suddenly lose my job because my company can't pay me anymore, and it is before I find a new job, we might have to cut back on vacations, eating out, and extra treats (or realistically whatever you will have to do), but we'll be fine. Taking care of you is my top priority, so don't worry!"

5

So, What Can You Really Tell Me about God?

In the upper elementary years, children become ever more fascinated with the idea of God and religion. This does not mean they become more religious. In fact, when children reach this stage, many parents report an increase in resistance to attending religious services ("It's sooooo boring") or religious school ("Can't I skip it just this once?"), which often doesn't ever abate for a number of different reasons we will discuss in this chapter.

Parents who believe strongly in a religious education often successfully resolve this resistance to (and eventual dislike of) religious school by choosing to send their children to full-time parochial schools, thereby avoiding the issue of their children having to attend religious school in addition to regular school. If you have a younger child, you should take a look at Chapter Five, "Little Kids Can

Be Spiritual," in *The Top 50 Questions Kids Ask (Pre-K through 2nd Grade)*, for a discussion about how to stem a dislike of religious school before it even begins.

Now, we're ready to tackle the questions!

#25: DOES GOD EXIST?
(OR: IS THERE A GOD?)

James was impressed when his daughter Caitlyn (age 9½), lying in bed just before falling asleep, asked him, "Daddy, is there really a God?"

"I wasn't exactly sure how to respond because it seemed like a deep question for such a young girl! I believe in God, so of course I said yes, but she didn't leave it at that. 'How do we know, Daddy? We can't see God.' She had a good point. I told her it was a big conversation that would have to wait until another time because it was time to go to sleep."

James is right; this is a big question and a big conversation. What is the best way to respond to your child's all-time biggest question about the existence of God, beyond yes or no, in a way that will help her grow both emotionally and cognitively?

Uncovering the Meaning

Religious leaders, philosophers, and just plain folks like you and me have been struggling with this question since—well, since forever it seems. So it is impressive that your elementary-school-age child is ready to tackle it too.

The concept of God captures your child's interest because it challenges her brain to think hard—is God real? It asks her to explore the depths of her heart and soul—am I a believer?

Older-elementary-age children are just beginning to develop the ability to think abstractly and philosophically. Although this skill will continue to grow through the middle-school and teen years, into adulthood, it is exciting to see the seedlings now.

As your child develops the skills of abstract thinking, she will question and challenge the status quo in many different arenas. On the subject of God, a clear response to her questions will help her become a less confused and more open-minded thinker. By answering her questions clearly, you will also help her negotiate through this confusing world of "no proof and no evidence," by guiding her in one of three ways:

- to believe in the existence of God
- to not believe in the existence of God
- to choose what she believes for herself

It is important to know that there is no right or wrong way to guide your child. Rather, providing a forum for open, nonjudgmental discussion and questioning *within your belief system* is the most important way to help her continue growing cognitively and emotionally.

The Best Way to Respond

I will begin by offering you one of my favorite psychological tips—one that I learned in graduate school and that I use almost every single day with my patients and with my own children in many different situations. Before giving your child a response, it will be useful for you to find out what she thinks the answer might be. This will help you determine how best to answer her. *Do this by answering a question with a question!* Therefore, before saying anything, solicit her opinion by asking, "Do *you* think God exists?" Then wait for a response.

If you believe your child should make up her own mind about God's existence, then all you have to do is enthusiastically validate whatever she says. But don't be surprised if she changes her belief system at least once or twice as she goes through different stages of development—particularly during adolescence.

If you are more comfortable with the idea of guiding your child toward your own belief system, then knowing how your child currently feels will help you in this task. For example, if you believe in God, but your child says, "I don't think God exists," you will need to be armed with a much more comprehensive response than you would if your child's beliefs are already consistent with your own. Nevertheless, it is important not to become upset, judgmental, critical, frustrated, or angry with your child if she does not immediately see things your way. You are much more likely to help her to eventually believe in God (or not, if this is your belief system), if you encourage her to do so in a supportive, patient, and encouraging manner.

Remember, dismissing her beliefs as trivial or wrong (even though they may seem so to you) is more likely to solidify them and push your child even further away from you and the ideals in which you believe.

#26: IF THERE IS A GOD, WHY DO BAD THINGS HAPPEN?
(OR: WHY DOES GOD LET WARS HAPPEN? IF GOD EXISTS, WHY ARE THERE POOR/SICK/HUNGRY PEOPLE IN THE WORLD? WHY DOES GOD LET PEOPLE HATE EACH OTHER?)

Paula shared the following touching story with me about her son Christopher (age 11): "Chris's friend's older brother was killed in a car accident—he was a passenger in a car with a drunk driver. Chris was very upset, more than we expected he would be. One day he asked me, 'Mom, how can God let someone die when they're still young? Maybe there really isn't a God.' It was hard to see him struggling so much with such confusing feelings."

It isn't unusual for children—or even adults—to wonder about how a "good" God could allow tragic things to happen. As with the previous question, it is one that many great minds have pondered and tried to resolve. I have no intention of even trying to compete with such learned and scholarly religious leaders and philosophers. Rather, I will help you understand the psychological reasons your child is beginning to ask this and similar questions now, and offer the best way to respond (always consistent with your belief system) in order to support your child's cognitive and emotional growth.

Uncovering the Meaning

Younger children tend not to question the existence of God. Rather, they are more curious about what God looks like, where God is, and other similar specifics—if you check out *The Top 50 Questions Kids Ask (Pre-K through 2nd Grade)*, you'll see what I mean. But for your older, now more philosophical child, it is becoming a whole different ball game.

For a child in the older elementary grades, the idea of God represents a possible "authority figure," sort of like a parent. When your child asks this question, he is wondering (using the newly forming abstract thinking part of his brain) how this supposedly "good parent" could allow bad things to happen to people.

It's a little scary to him to imagine that this powerful "parent," who he can't even see, might have such leverage over everyone—and not only over children, but even over adults. For some children (and adults) it is a lot easier—and even more logical—to think that perhaps God does not exist, because a good God, like a good parent, would not allow such bad things to happen.

If you do not believe in God and do not bring your child up to believe in God either, this is a closed case for you.

However, if you do believe in God and want your child to do so as well, this question presents a complex dilemma for your child and one to which you need to respond with respect, in order to help your child negotiate the confusion he is experiencing.

Again, I remind you that I will not be tackling this from a deeply religious or philosophical angle. Truthfully, I don't think a complex explanation is necessary in order to satisfy an elementary-age child. In fact, I believe it might scare your child.

Rather, a developmentally appropriate explanation that does not provoke fear will effectively help your child understand how the existence of God does not preclude bad things from happening. Your response should take into account that your child thinks of God as a "good parent" and is confused that God would disappoint or hurt his "children." This offers an opportunity for you to introduce your child to the concept that parents create their children, but then children are responsible for their own actions.

The Best Way to Respond

The best way to respond to this question is with a version of the following: "You were born from my body, right? You grew in my body and I created you. But that doesn't mean that I have complete control over every choice that you make in your life. You think for yourself and choose for yourself. You decide whom you are going to be friends with and whom you don't like. You decide if you're going to work hard in school or slack off. Well, it's sort of the same with God. God created the beautiful earth and all the people, and then God stepped back and let us decide how we are going to live our lives. We choose to be nice to each other or not. We choose to get in a car with a drunk driver or not. We choose to make wars or not. It is not God's fault. Sometimes sad things happen to people, like illness or dying from being old, because we are human beings and our bodies aren't perfect. But most of the time, we have choices and we have to make good choices. *People have to take responsibility for their own behavior—grown-ups do, and so do kids*." This last sentence is the most important life lesson you can teach your child—now and at any time, ever!

#27: IS THERE REALLY A HELL?

Judy and Allen's nine-year-old twins Sierra and Macy are worried about hell—who can blame them! Judy explained, "Sometimes the girls are afraid to go to sleep at night because they are scared of having nightmares about hell. They can't even articulate what exactly they're afraid of—just somewhere 'creepy' you go when you die if you've done bad things. But they are not clear about how bad you need to be to end up in hell. We've told them over and over again that they are good girls and not to worry about it."

Do you think there is a hell? Are you absolutely sure? So how do you respond to this question?

Uncovering the Meaning

For those who believe in hell—adults and children alike—it is not a fun concept to anticipate and surely a place one works hard to avoid.

But, for a child, the idea of hell can be even more frightening, because even if her parents don't believe in it, she may hear friends and even other adults talking about it. At this age your child is old enough to pay attention to and understand these conversations and begin thinking seriously about them. In addition, the word "hell" is thrown about as slang so frequently that she may well wonder about its existence, despite what her parents tell her.

Whether or not you believe in hell, it is tempting to sidestep the issue and avoid answering this question because it is a difficult concept to explain, and potentially a scary one. The problem with taking this route is that it won't stop your child from wondering about hell. She will create her own answer to the question using her imagination, and she will develop a fantasy of hell, which is likely to be much scarier than any explanation you could (or should) give her. Therefore, as difficult as it may be, this is a question to tackle head-on, making sure to help your child quell any fears that may be lurking.

The Best Way to Respond

If you don't believe in hell, you can simply say so. However, keep in mind that you child may still wonder and ask about it, given that it is such a commonly spoken-of concept.

If you believe in hell, or you are not sure, you can't tell your child with assurance that it doesn't exist. By this age it won't take long for your child to recognize that your response isn't authentic in its reflection of your belief system. On the other hand, you don't want to scare your child, so you need to give her a response that serves two purposes:

1. It offers her reassurance and reduces fear and anxiety.
2. It gives her clear, easy, concrete rules that, when followed, will ensure that she will not end up in hell.

A response to this question could be a variation of the following. Of course you should change your response so that it fits your belief system, "No one knows for absolutely sure if hell exists. But if it does, a person only goes there if she does something very, very bad—like kill someone or break into someone's house and steal something. You don't go to hell for doing things when you're a child, even if they are things that make your mom or dad angry. You might get into trouble for bad behavior, or for doing something you shouldn't, or even for being rude or getting a bad grade in school because you didn't study. But you don't go to hell for those things. People can only go to hell for very bad grown-up behavior. Your job is to keep on working hard in school and being a good friend and a good sister and being respectful. As long as you work at doing all the things you are supposed to, you don't have to worry about going to hell, even if you get into trouble sometimes."

Including all the above factors is important, because a fear of hell should not be used as a way to convince your child to behave. This will terrify her and make her hate religion. It will also cause her to resent you and cause her to slowly grow to believe that you don't have the ability to manage her behavior without holding this fear over her head. She will then lose respect for you, particularly if, at some point in her life, she decides that hell doesn't exist.

#28: WHERE DO GRANDMA AND GRANDPA GO AFTER THEY DIE?

Bridgette, mother of Toby (age 10), thought her son seemed more curious than upset when he asked her this question. But she wanted to respond in a way that *wouldn't* upset him. She just wasn't sure how to do this successfully. "I didn't want to scare Toby, and I also didn't want to tell him something I wasn't completely sure about. So I told him that they go to heaven. That didn't really satisfy him though, because after thinking about it for a second or two he said, 'But what happens there?' I was stumped!"

Children begin to think about death when they are very young (especially if they experience it firsthand). Of course, like everyone, they have fears related to death, and we will discuss these in Chapter Four. But as your child grows up, he also develops a curiosity about death, somewhat unrelated to being fearful. This interest is often particularly piqued when someone very close to your child dies during these years—like a grandparent. He might also ask this question when a beloved pet dies.

As difficult as it may be for you to discuss death (and what happens after death) with your child, it is important for you to do so in order to help him sort through this confusing stage.

Uncovering the Meaning

As you know, children are curious about everything. Therefore, it is perfectly normal for your child to want to understand exactly what happens to a person's body or soul after the person dies.

But before you launch into a big explanation, you need to clarify exactly what your child is asking. It isn't necessary—or recommended—to give him any more information than he is specifically wondering about right now. For example, your child might be curious about what happens to a person's body after death. If your response includes information about what happens to the soul, he may become distressed or confused with too much information.

The best way to ensure that you are not answering the wrong question or *more* than you should, is to go back to my favorite tip: answer a question with a question. In this case, when your child asks you his question, you can respond by asking, "Where do you think a person goes?" What he says next will tip you off as to how to best respond to him in a way that will offer him comfort as well as make sense to him.

The Best Way to Respond

As we have discussed, first you need to clarify whether your child is wondering where someone *physically* goes after dying or where his soul may go (given that you believe in heaven or an afterlife).

If your child wants to know what happens to the physical body of a person, it is important to be honest but not graphic enough to scare your child. For example, you might say, "When someone dies he is placed in a long box called a coffin, and the coffin is put in the ground in the cemetery and buried. A stone is put next to the place where the coffin is buried to remember where it is. We've driven by a cemetery before. Next time I'll point one out to you, and you'll see what I mean." I wouldn't say more than this unless your child asks questions. In fact, children in this age range don't need to know information about what a dead person looks like, whether or not he is dressed, how deeply he is buried, or anything else—even if he asks. Sometimes fulfilling this type of morbid curiosity can scare a child in a way that neither you nor he would have anticipated at the time. This sort of fear can linger for months or even longer. Instead of responding to these types of detailed questions, I would recommend that you say you don't think he needs to know any more right now and when he is a bit older you can talk about it again.

When your child is more curious about what happens to a person's soul or spirit after death, you will need to think carefully about your response. Since the concepts to be discussed—heaven, the soul—are already intangible, it is easy to slip into euphemisms when discussing these with your child. For example, responses like "They go 'up there'" or "They're always watching you" are vague yet seem satisfying to you. But for an elementary-age child, they are actually not satisfying at all and, in fact, may be confusing and cause anxiety.

More than one child I have known has thought that a deceased grandparent was living in the attic, after being told by a parent that he or she was "up there"! Other children wonder if their now-departed relatives are watching them take showers, use the bathroom, or write in their private diaries, because they are "always watching you."

When you talk to your child about where a deceased person has "gone," the key is to be concrete and clear—which is admittedly difficult to do about this particular topic. Your goal is to make sure your child feels that the deceased person is safe and happy, *particularly* if the ending of his or her life was less than peaceful or if your child is asking this question in advance of an old or dying person's death.

Your explanation can certainly include the idea that the person is "watching over" your child, but this should be in a limited, rather than an intrusive (or, as my three kids like to say, "stalkerish") way. Your explanation might be similar to the following, but of course you should tailor it to fit the specific needs of your family and your belief system: "Grandma and Grandpa go to heaven after they die. Heaven is a peaceful and happy place. They will always look down on you and be with you on special occasions, like your birthday and graduation, and you will have them in your heart all the time."

#29: WHY DO I HAVE TO GO TO [FILL IN YOUR RELIGIOUS SERVICE] AND PRAY, EVEN IF I DON'T WANT TO?

Hillary wants the family to attend religious services regularly, but Laura (age 9½) complains every week. "She gets so indignant," sighed Hillary, "and spends the entire time complaining so much that it ruins the experience for the rest of the family. She tells me she hates it, it's boring, she doesn't believe in God, no one else has to go—every excuse she can think of!"

Many parents wonder if it is really worth the effort to force their children to attend religious services when they are so adamantly against it. Perhaps they will come around when they're a bit older? What do you think?

Uncovering the Meaning

Battles over religious observance are common between parents and children of all ages. In fact, if you take a look at *The Top 50 Questions Kids Ask (Pre-K through 2nd Grade)*, you'll see that I address this issue there too, but, of course, from a slightly different angle.

As we have been discussing throughout this book, your older-elementary-age child is beginning to think more and more independently. She may believe that she is old enough to make all her own choices and decisions, but, of course, she is not! She may not be happy with all the choices you are making for her, particularly if they are different from the decisions that some of friends' parents make. If attending religious services is not popular among her peers—if most of them are playing soccer or hanging out on the block—she will resent attending even more. But, if it important to your family, this isn't a good reason for her *not* to go! If all the other parents allowed their children to watch R-rated movies, would you? I hope not! It's not good for your child's emotional health. For this same reason, if you have determined that it is good for your child—and your family—to attend services regularly, you can and should make it clear to your child that you expect her to attend—without complaint.

In fact, you are right if you have determined that it is good for your child to attend religious services—probably for different reasons than you think. Research has shown that teens who are religious are much less likely to smoke cigarettes, drink alcohol, or use illegal drugs.

Sometimes a child is reluctant to attend religious services because both her parents are not in agreement about their importance. Perhaps one parent would like the family to attend services more regularly, but the other parent is not as invested. If this sounds like your family, it is very important that you and your partner come to a compromise that meets both your needs as well as meets the needs of your child, *and* that doesn't send your child mixed messages.

When your family does attend religious services, it doesn't yet matter if your child chooses to formally pray or not. At this age, she should understand that attending religious services is an important family activity in which participation is required. Aside from the spiritual aspect of religion, there is, for children, also a ritualistic, habit-forming aspect of it. Very often, a child's belief in God and her spirituality both develop *after* she has cultivated a core knowledge and familiarity with her religion.

If your child misses the opportunity to create the blueprint for religious observance in elementary school, it likely won't happen in middle or high school because you won't suddenly be able to insist that a child of that age attends services with you. Therefore, if you don't insist that your child goes with you, it is highly unlikely that her desire to do so will ever change. In addition, if you don't insist that your child attends services with you, the message you will inadvertently be communicating is that it isn't important to you that she attend.

If you believe in religion and you want your child to do so too, this is an important battle to fight. In addition, do so because it offers one more form of inoculation against illegal substance use and abuse as your child gets older, as well as a guarantee of a few moments of peaceful family time in our fast-paced, always stressful world.

The Best Way to Respond

Your response to this question should actually be no different from your response to any other question your child asks about a topic that is of paramount importance to you.

Imagine your child was asking you, "Why do I have to go to school if I don't want to?" "Why do I have to go brush my teeth if I don't want to?" "Why do I have to eat healthy food if I don't want to?" Each of these questions has a logical answer: "You do these things because they are good for your health and because it's the rule in our family." You should base your response to the question on this premise.

Your response may sound similar to the one that follows. Of course you should adapt it to fit your needs. In some cases it is okay to allow your child to bring a book to read or a quiet activity in which to engage. Although this isn't technically participating, it may be a way to get a reluctant child to begin moving in the right direction. "You need to go to services because it is a very important part of our family life. You get to do lots of things that you like to do, and sometimes you have to do the things that I want to do because they make me and our family happy. You don't have a choice about this, but we can talk about how to make you like it more. While you are there, you can pray any way you want, or think about anything you want that makes you feel good and peaceful. But you can't complain or whine or behave inappropriately. If you do, there will be a consequence."

6

Sibling Stuff

If you have more than one child, I bet you have experienced sibling rivalry to one degree or another. It's not fun, but in reality the competition, jealousy, teasing, and out-and-out wars prepare your child for the world outside your home, helping her develop resilience and skills for managing similar, inevitable social experiences. In fact, having siblings helps a child to adjust to sharing, being flexible, and relating within a peer group that much sooner. Of course single children learn all this too—with cousins and friends—it just takes a little longer and a bit more planning by parents to ensure regular exposure to other children.

As the parent of a single—or any—child, you also need to make sure you don't always take the side of your own child when it comes to helping him negotiate sticky situations. This will go a long way toward enabling him to develop the skills he may otherwise learn as the member of a sibling group. You can review Chapter Two, Question #8, for some tips on not always taking your child's side when he is in an argument or fight with another child.

Despite its practical utility for your child's social life, sibling rivalry can be stressful for parents and children. Notwithstanding the period after the birth of a second child (which represents the quintessential time that a child is jealous of a sibling), the older-elementary years are often a time when sibling rivalry peaks. This is because many older-elementary-age children—now more confident and with stronger verbal skills—are willing to assert their displeasure with both older and younger siblings far more readily than they might have when they were younger and less verbal.

Parents sometimes exacerbate sibling rivalry without even realizing it, by accidentally comparing siblings to each other, mixing them up, or inadvertently treating them "unfairly" in the eyes of their siblings. It is practically impossible to escape the "it's not fair's" and "you like her more's." The most common questions that children ask on the topic of siblings all reflect sibling rivalry in one form or another. So let's jump right in and begin to explore the issues, and come up with the solutions.

#30: WHY IS SHE ALLOWED TO STAY UP LATER AND I HAVE TO GO TO SLEEP EARLIER?
(OR: WHY DO WE HAVE TO GO TO SLEEP AT THE SAME TIME IF I'M OLDER?)

Ashley (age 8) gives her parents, Penny and Sherman, a hard time every night because she doesn't understand why her older brother Cole (age 10) has the privilege of going to go to sleep an hour later than her. "It's not fair!" declares Ashley. "Cole and I wake up at the same time every day for school. He's not so much older than me—he's also in elementary school. Why can't we go to sleep at the same time?"

Bedtime is often a challenge for parents, because very few kids want to go to bed at the designated bedtime—no matter when that may be. When siblings bicker with each other and, more often, with you over who gets to stay up later, it complicates a situation that may already be fraught with stress and arguments. It is therefore important to learn to understand your children's concerns and set guidelines for them so they stop feeling upset and jealous.

Uncovering the Meaning
To a child, bedtime is like a form of valuable currency. The later she can go to bed, the "richer" she considers

herself. (Of course, it is not in a child's best interest to go to sleep too late, so effectively setting limits in this area is important. If you're still struggling with this, *The Top 50 Questions Kids Ask (Pre-K through 2nd Grade)* gives you tips on how to do it.) It's therefore not surprising that siblings will battle mightily over who gets to stay up later—even if it is only by a few minutes. It makes sense to you—an adult—that older siblings get to stay up later, but for children, like Ashley, it doesn't always seem logical.

Typically, if your elementary-school-age child has a sibling that is much older (high-school age, for example), she won't argue about having an earlier bedtime. This seems logical to her. She may not even argue about going to bed earlier than a sibling in middle school. But if her sibling is only a bit older than she is, or if she's the older one, you already know that you have a difficult battle on your hands.

Nevertheless, bedtime is not your child's decision to make. There are several issues to consider when establishing bedtimes for your children. The privilege of giving a later bedtime to an older child is one of these issues. But it is not the only one, and in some families should not even be *the* issue that determines the bedtime routine. The other factors to consider are as follows:

- How much sleep each child needs (this is not age-dependent; a younger child may need less, while an older child might require more). You can determine this by how easily each child falls asleep at night and wakes up in the morning, and then how well she functions during the day with a given amount of sleep.

- In some homes it is less chaotic and more manageable to stagger bath and bedtimes, while in others it is easier to put all children to bed in one quick sweep of hugs and kisses (especially if they share a room).

- Does staggering bedtimes routines (reading, snuggling) allow you much needed time alone with each child, or is this particular part of your relationship with your child well satisfied?

- If you have several children, it is not "all or none"; if it is best for your schedule, some bedtimes can be staggered and some can be together (ensuring that *all* your children will be unhappy with you!)

As you can see, although your child may think only about how unfair it is that she can't stay up as late as an older sibling, or that she has to go to sleep at the same time as a younger sibling, she does not take into account all these other important concerns. You, on the other hand, need to do so, or your child will be sleep-deprived, and your schedule will constantly be topsy-turvy.

At the same time, though, you will find yourself locked in fewer battles if you acknowledge how valuable bedtime is to your child—remember, she considers it as precious as gold or gems! Pitting one sibling against another, at least in her eyes, makes the battle even more worthwhile. A form of compromise may therefore be necessary, in order to lessen the bickering and feelings of unfairness. This does not mean that you have to give up on what is best for your children's health or your family's routine.

The Best Way to Respond

Begin by deciding what is best for your children and your family—whether this is staggered bedtimes or not. Next, build in a compromise that allows each of them to feel happier.

Example #1—If you decide that staggered bedtimes are best because you like the idea of the older child having a privilege, or it gives you time with each child alone, say to your older child: "You are allowed to go to sleep later because you are older, but you are not allowed to brag about it or hold it over your sister's head in any way. If I see you do that, the privilege will be taken away."

Say to your younger child, "You go to sleep earlier because you are younger, and when you are your brother's age, you will get to go to sleep later too. When he was your age, he went to sleep earlier. *But*, on weekends, or any night that there isn't school the next day, you can go to sleep at the same time as him. If you whine and complain about it, I will think that you're not being mature about it, and I will take away that privilege of staying up later on weekends."

Example #2—If you decide that your children should

go to bed simultaneously because it makes your nighttime routine less complex, or because you feel that your older child needs the additional sleep, there is probably no need to say anything to your younger child. But to your older child, say something similar to the following: "Everyone's body needs a certain amount of sleep, and it doesn't have to do with how old they are. If you don't get the amount you need, your brain and body will be too tired to do well in school or in sports or in all your other activities. Getting enough sleep isn't a privilege related to being older; it is my job to make sure you get what you need. But, if you don't complain, whine, and act immaturely about it, you can stay up half an hour later than your sister on the weekends and any days that there isn't school the next day. If you do give me a hard time about it, I will take away that privilege because you will be letting me know that you aren't acting older and more maturely."

#31: WHY DOES HE [A YOUNGER SIBLING] GET TO SPEND SO MUCH TIME WITH YOU?
(OR: WHY DOES HE ALWAYS GET TO SNUGGLE WITH YOU?)

Almost every day, Timothy (age 8) asks his mom, Diana, why his younger brother Connor (age 3½) gets to spend so much time with her. "I feel really guilty sometimes," explained Diana. "Timmy is really jealous of the time I have with Connor while he is in school. I remind him that Connor is in school for part of the day too, and that all we do is run errands anyway. But it doesn't seem to help. And now I'm pregnant—what is he going to do when there is another child also taking my attention?"

As I described in the opening of this chapter, the older elementary years can be the time that children most acutely experience sibling rivalries and jealousies. It is because they start to think a lot about all the different ways that they *can* be jealous! This type of sibling jealousy is one of the most common. Let's take a look at why this is, and what you can do about it.

Uncovering the Meaning

By this stage, your child is old enough—and smart enough—to think about what is going on at home while he is not there, and he knows that he doesn't like feeling left out. In fact, he may have begun to experience this jealousy when he and his sibling were younger, but unless he was very verbal, he might not have been able to articulate his feelings well enough to explain them to you. (Remember, all development is on a continuum; some children will reach milestones earlier and some later. You should consider your child normal unless he is very far off the continuum. If you are worried, you can speak to your child's doctor.)

It is normal for an older sibling to feel pangs of jealousy when he has to go off to school, leaving a parent home with a younger child. In fact, as your older child becomes more and more independent, he experiences a conflict. He loves the feeling of growing up, but at the same time he misses the particular type of closeness he had with his mom or dad when he was much younger.

Observing this closeness between his parent and younger sibling (little kids spend more time with parents; they cuddle and snuggle more; they cry and so are comforted more) can make an older child feel jealous, and even a little worried that you love your younger child more than you love him. This conflict—wanting to grow up, while wanting to hold on to the intimacy of babyhood that he sees daily—is the root of the jealousy and the question. It is a struggle that will continue for years, reaching its peak during adolescence, when your child will be faced with the choice between childhood and adulthood. By helping him through it now, for the first time, you will ease his way when he goes through it at this later stage.

But first, ask yourself the following question: *Are you providing enough snuggles, alone time, and comforting moments for your older child?* Or have you inadvertently pushed him into the role of "big brother" now that you have a younger child—or perhaps even more than one. Do you expect him to be the "grown-up" one in your family? Perhaps your older child is right to be feeling that he is not getting enough "babying." It is easy to allow an older child to slip into this role. Once we have a younger child, especially a baby, it is easy for our perspective to shift. We forget that an eight-, nine-, or even ten-year-old child usually still needs to be hugged or cuddled, even when he seems so independent and grown-up—especially when compared to a younger child.

In addition, sometimes a parent may feel a little hurt or rejected when an older child wants to spend more time with peers and on activities and less time with you. It is then easy to focus more attention on a younger sibling, who is still fully reliant on mom or dad. You may then accidentally push your older child into a more grown-up role for which he may not be ready. However, your older-elementary-age child still needs you just as much. He just needs you in a slightly different way than he did before. His jealousy and questions tell you this.

You will be happy to know that you are *not* a bad parent if you have fallen into the trap of expecting your older child to grow up before he is ready to do so. It is easy to resolve this issue as well as address the issue of jealousy that provokes the question.

The Best Way to Respond

You can best help your child by showing him that he doesn't have to choose between you being nurturing and him becoming more independent—he can and should have both. He needs you to show him that his jealousy is unwarranted, because he is able to begin growing up and still be close to you, while his younger sibling isn't yet old enough to take on the excitement of independence.

First, it is most helpful to your child if you begin your response by *acknowledging his feelings*, rather than denying the issue. *Instead of saying,* "I don't spend more time with Connor; he's in school for part of the day anyway," *it is better to say,* "I bet you feel upset thinking I spend more time with Connor. I'm glad that you're telling me about your feelings, so now we can do something about it."

Your child will be much more likely to share his feelings with you—about this and anything else—if you *acknowledge his feelings as real and valid.*

Second, your goal is to show your child that there is a solution to the problem that will result in him feeling that he has more time with you while still being a "big kid." Some solutions include the following:

- Carving out time alone with your older child when another adult can take your younger child(ren) (the other parent, relative, baby-sitter).
- Taking your child out of school once in a while for lunch while your other child is in school or with a sitter. This is a *very* effective way of making an older child feel special, and any elementary-school-age child is still young enough that this won't be academically disruptive, even in the oldest grades.
- Giving your older child a later bedtime (see Question #30) so that you have time together with

no interruptions, or allowing your older child to stay up later than his regular bedtime once a week to spend special time with you.

- Taking only your older child with you to run weekend or evening errands (this is not a good option if you're a single parent, unless you have baby-sitting help).

- Going into work late once in a while to have breakfast with your older child, but sending your younger one(s) to school, with the sitter, or to daycare.

- Grabbing small opportunities to spend time with your child (while the baby is napping, when your younger child is playing with someone else or engaged in a TV show). Tell your child you *want* to spend this time with him.

- Reminding him that you're proud of how grown up he is, but you still want him to snuggle and cuddle with you!

#32: CAN WE SEND MY BROTHER/SISTER SOMEWHERE [BOARDING SCHOOL/JAIL/TO LIVE WITH SOMEONE ELSE]?

Carla's daughter Mariah (age 9) gets so frustrated with her brothers, Oscar (age 10½) and Eddie (age 13), that she routinely asks her mom if they can be sent somewhere else. "I think Mariah would like to be an only child," sighed Carla. "She asks me all the time if one or both of her brothers can go and live with a cousin or with one of their friends—even for a little while."

In anger, kids will say all sorts of things about their siblings. How much of it is true, and how much is momentary frustration? And what's the best way for you to respond? Should you exhibit understanding and sympathy or offer a reprimand for being mean? Let's explore this question to find out.

Uncovering the Meaning

There are several different reasons for a child to feel she would like a sibling to "go elsewhere." If your child consistently expresses this type of wish about a sibling, it likely stems from underlying feelings of hurt, insecurity, or resentment. Some of the most common reasons for this are listed below. Of course every family situation is different, so your child may have a slightly different reason for resenting her sibling , including the following:

- a brand-new baby who evokes jealousy
- an older sibling who is *very* bossy and overpowering
- a younger sibling who is cute and gets *a lot* of attention
- a twin sibling—because it can be difficult to share one's entire life with another person
- a sibling (usually older) who bullies, teases, or torments

- two siblings of the same gender who make a third feel left out or ganged up on (this may be how Mariah feels, especially since she is also the youngest)
- a sibling who is smarter/more athletic/more popular/thinner/better-looking and therefore makes a child feel inadequate (despite parental reassurance of the opposite)
- a sibling who gets extra attention due to having a disability or illness (even something relatively minor)

Once you understand the cause of your child's negative feelings toward her sibling, it is far easier to address these feelings. Although it is unpleasant to hear a child wish that a brother or sister lived elsewhere, it is not helpful to address this issue in anger. Rather, if you recognize this question as a sign that your children need help mending their relationship with each other, you can facilitate this, rather than being angry that your child is letting you know how she feels.

The Best Way to Respond

When your child asks this question (or any variation of it), it is best to refrain from expressing disapproval or anger. Rather, you will learn a lot by asking your child to tell you exactly what is causing her feelings. However, be patient when she talks to you, because her reason may not be immediately clear-cut or easy to understand—even to herself. This is because *children can't always identify the reasons for their feelings*. It may take more than one conversation to understand your child's feelings. You may also need to spend some time observing your children's interactions with each other to really learn what might be upsetting one child.

Although you do not want to respond to this question in a critical or angry way, it *is* appropriate to help your child learn to express her feelings in a manner that is more constructive and less hurtful to her sibling. What's more, you can explain to her that wishing her sibling would go away is simply not a practical solution. In fact, she also needs to hear that she may be contributing to the rift between herself and her sibling. An explanation similar to the following would be helpful: "I'm so glad that you have told me what is bothering you. Now, instead of you always wishing your brother would go away, we can do something to make you feel better about having a brother. We will talk to him, and we will all work together to make things better between you and him, so that you won't feel so angry and sad. It won't happen right away, but we will work on it a little at a time. But don't be surprised if he says there are things he would like you to change too. That's the way relationships work—everyone has to compromise."

#33: WHY DO YOU ALWAYS GET OUR NAMES WRONG?
(OR: SHOULD WE WEAR NAME TAGS? WHY DO YOU ALWAYS MIX UP OUR NAMES? WHY DON'T YOU KNOW WHO WE ARE?)

Ingrid and Jim have a very busy home! They admit to sometimes—well, often—mixing up the names of their four children, Jesse (age 13), Jenna (age 10), Olivia (age 8), and Corey (age 8). An outspoken Jenna was the spokesperson for the kids. "My parents always get us mixed up. My mom will start to call one of us and then halfway through realize she's calling the wrong one and switch to another one and then switch again. The other day she called me Jesse—he's a boy!"

This was one of the most frequently submitted questions. It came in many different forms, from parents all over, so if you suffer from this problem, which I have named Name Confusion Syndrome (NCS), you need not worry that perhaps you are getting senile—it is normal! I have to admit that my husband and I too suffer from NCS, exasperating our children with name mix-ups on occasion. However, the instance that stands out most in the minds of all my children (and they remind my husband and me of it frequently) was a few years ago when my husband—a more loving and dedicated father you will never find—looked at our son Max and called him Sam. We do not have a Sam anywhere in our family—not even a pet! To this day, none of us have a clue where that name came from.

Uncovering the Meaning

Despite the fact that it is perfectly normal sometimes to mix up your children's names, they may not see it the same way as you do. Furthermore if your name mix-ups happen more than occasionally, your children may feel insulted and upset by it. Consider how you would feel if someone close to you regularly got your name wrong—not very happy, right?

Sometimes a child also becomes upset because he believes—incorrectly—that your mix-up is the result of more than you simply making a mistake. He jumps to the conclusion that there is something about him that is so similar to his sibling that it is causing you to confuse them. Since it is important to him to be seen by others as a unique individual, this notion is distressing to him. If you have twins, or even children of the same gender that are very close in age, this issue may become exacerbated because their sense of individual identity could be even more greatly challenged.

It is less likely for parents to confuse the names of children who are different genders, but when they do, it is even more distressing to a child. This is under-standable, because a child might begin to wonder if you see a quality in him that makes you think of the opposite sex.

Let's divert for a minute and consider this:

Having a strong identification with one's own gender is important to a child during this stage of development because boys and girls tend to gravitate, each to his own gender. For the most part, boys play with boys and girls with girls. Games, activities, and toys tend to be split along these same lines too—this is particularly clear during recess at school. Birthday parties also become a "one gender" affair. This is a normal part of growing up as a child reinforces his own gender-identity and bonds with peers.

Of course, as with everything we discuss, the rules are not hard and fast—there is a range of normal. This means that some boys like to play with girls, and some girls like to play with boys. However, if you are worried that your child's behavior seems to be *very* different from all the other children his age, it is a good idea to talk to your child's doctor, a child psychologist, or other mental health professional that specializes in children.

Now back to Name Confusion Syndrome. How should you handle NCS so that your children will not feel that you don't think they are all one child, and that you don't really care about their individual identities? How are you supposed to manage your own normal inability to get their names straight? *Should* they wear name tags?

The Best Way to Respond

I quite like the name tag idea, except that sometimes my children aren't directly in front of me when I'm confusing their names—I'm usually calling for them from another room. Perhaps I need a picture and name chart posted in each room—that might help!

Seriously, if your children complain that you confuse their names, it is possible that you too suffer from NCS. Admission is the first step toward recovery.

Next, you need to take three steps to reduce the stress your NCS may be causing your children:

1. Explain to them that your confusion has nothing to do with you thinking that they are in any way similar to each other. Give them concrete examples of the ways that you see them as unique.

2. Tell them that you will work toward confusing their names less often, but explain that you can't promise that you will be able to stop doing it completely right away (or ever). Tell them that you will check in with them to see how you are doing.

3. Reduce your NCS by pausing for a couple of seconds (or more if necessary) each time you are about to call one of your children. Think about the name you are about to say, and make sure it is the correct name. This will dramatically reduce the number of mistakes you make! As an extra bonus, you may also find that giving yourself those few extra seconds also reduces

the amount of impulsive yelling in which you might engage.

#34: HOW COME YOU LET HER STAY UP LATER/HAVE A COOKIE/WATCH TV/EAT IN THE DEN/GO TO SCHOOL LATE/PLAY WITH A FRIEND/[FILL IN YOUR OWN] AND YOU WON'T LET ME?

Annette feels that she is always negotiating with and explaining decisions to her daughter Kayla (age 8) because she is jealous of her sister Vanessa (age 10½). "Kayla always feels I treat Vanessa more fairly," explained Annette. "It's a losing battle because no matter what I say or do, it's not right!"

"It's not fair!" is one of the battle cries of childhood. And it is a tough one for a parent to negotiate. It can sometimes be difficult to be sure if you are being fair and equitable with your children—especially when their needs seem to be completely different. So, how can you be sure that you are doing the right thing? Let's figure it out.

Uncovering the Meaning

It is always best to begin by evaluating whether your child's complaint is accurate. In *some* cases, a child has a distorted view of whether her parent treats her fairly or not. Perhaps your child is jealous of her sibling for another reason. Rather than acknowledging this jealousy, she displaces it by blaming you. Maybe Kayla is jealous because Vanessa is becoming more social and not spending as much time with her. Kayla may not even be aware of the reason for her feelings, but knows that she is angry with Vanessa. Her anger comes out as a feeling that Vanessa is favored.

In other instances, both (or all) of your children feel like you're always treating the other more fairly. This is a sure sign that you're treating all of them (or none of them) fairly.

However, if one of your children consistently feels that she is treated differently from the other(s), it could be true. There are many reasons that you may be letting one child but not another engage in an activity. The most obvious of these (although a younger sibling may not like it) is that there are many things an older sibling gets to do that a younger sibling can't yet do (like walk to school alone, have a cell phone, go to the mall—the list goes on). In addition, a complaint heard just as frequently from older siblings is that younger siblings get to do things *earlier* in life than the older sibling did. For example, "How come she gets a cell phone when she's ten? I didn't get one until I was twelve." Or "Why do you let her stay up until 9 p.m.? When I was her age I had to go to sleep at 8:30."

The explanation (not that it will satisfy your child) is that for many people, parenting first children tends to be more "by the book." This is neither good nor bad, but it does tend to be less relaxed, less flexible parenting. By the time a second (or third) child comes around, you are a more relaxed, more adaptable parent—which is good (unless you were too relaxed and flexible to begin with; kids *do* need structure). In addition, having more than one child makes it more difficult to be as rigid as you may have been with one child—you don't have the time or energy. Your subsequent children benefit from this greater flexibility and more relaxed parenting. Your first-born sees it as "unfair." She tends to forget that she was the first to "blaze the way," experiencing practically everything before her younger sibling, and that she still has privileges that the younger child won't get until she is older.

Another situation that kids often describe as unfair is when a parent allows a son to engage in activities that a daughter of a similar age is not allowed to experience due to a fear for her safety. Angelica (age 10) is furious with her parents because they won't let her walk six blocks home from school. "Why can't I walk home?" she demands. "You let Chase (age 14) when he was my age. It's *so* not fair!"

Angelica's mom, Anna, sees the situation differently. "Chase is a boy. Even at ten, he was much bigger and stronger than Angelica. She is petite and pretty. I don't care what she says—crazy people are much more likely to abduct an adorable little girl walking alone than a ten-year-old boy. I don't care that to her it seems like—or *is*—a double-standard. I care about her safety."

You might be surprised to find out that a comprehensive study of missing children undertaken by the U.S. Department of Justice (published in 2002), does not fully support Anna's perspective. To begin, although she is right that girls are more likely to be abducted than boys, it does not mean that boys are safe. In fact, of the 58,200 children abducted by nonfamily members during the year of this study, only 65 percent were girls. Perhaps, at ten years old, Anna should not have let Chase walk to school alone either. In addition, no matter how much taller or tougher Chase may have been compared to Angelica, the truth is that any child, when confronted with a weapon, is equally vulnerable to abduction.

Here's another interesting fact. *More children (girls and boys) are abducted by someone with whom they are familiar than by a complete stranger.* This emphasizes the critical need to teach your children *not only* about stranger danger, but also *about never going anywhere with anyone, unless a parent or caregiver has given them permission to do so*—even with someone they know well, such as a neighbor or friend, and even if that person is asking the child for help.

The study also revealed that *teenage girls* are, by far, the most likely victims of abduction (by sexual predators).

Practicing a double standard is, therefore, not such a bad idea. However, do so not when your child is young, since both genders are potential victims at that age, but rather as your daughter gets older. Your daughter may not like this idea, but Anna is right about this: your daughter's safety is what is most important!

Yet another reason parents sometimes treat siblings differently has to do with their levels of maturity, or their developmental, social, or learning needs. For example, Kyle (age 7) has attention deficit hyperactivity disorder (ADHD), which causes him to have poor impulse control. His dad, Charles, definitely doesn't want him eating in the den! But Charlie Jr. (age 8½) is careful, calm, and neat. Charles is fine with him eating in the den occasionally. "It's not fair!" exclaims Kyle. "How come he gets to eat in the den and I don't?" Later that night, while their dad was putting them to bed, Kyle had a meltdown. "You're always nicer to Charlie! How come he can do everything and I can't do anything?" he cried. Charles felt terrible.

In situations like this, you sometimes have to meet the needs of your more complex child, rather than your easier one. At times, your easier child may not even realize she is compromising: the family rule can simply be "no eating in the den." At other times, the need for concessions should be made clear: Charlie can be helped to be patient with Kyle, rather than getting mad at him whenever he knocks something over. This is part of living in a family. At the same time, in order to minimize the chance of resentment between siblings, you always need to be careful that you are not putting too much of a burden on one sibling to compromise for another sibling.

The Best Way to Respond

Begin by determining the reason for your child's question. This will help you address your child's feelings. However, no matter what the reason for your child's question, the core of your response needs to communicate the following two points to your child:

1. Tell your child that in your family *everyone gets what they need.*

2. Then explain that getting what you need doesn't mean you will always get the same thing as every other person. In fact, there will be times when your child and her sibling won't get the same thing. This is not a reason to be jealous. It simply means that they don't need the same thing right now. As a parent, it is important for you to believe this. It is your job to meet the needs of your children. Their needs will not be the same. While you should treat your children fairly, you should not feel compelled to treat them in exactly the same way at all times.

For example you may say, "Kayla, I'm sorry that you feel I treat Vanessa better than you. However, in our family *everyone gets what they need.* That means sometimes you get something and Vanessa doesn't, or she gets something and you don't. That may be time spent with you, something bought for you, or something given to you. I will keep reminding you of this until you feel comfortable that I love both of you equally, but that doesn't mean I will treat you exactly the same all the time."

Another example may be similar to the following: "Angelica, I know you feel it is unfair that Chase was allowed to walk to school at your age. However, the circumstances were different when Chase was younger. He walked to school with a large group of boys every day and was never alone. That is not the same as you wanting to walk to school alone, or occasionally with another girl when she happens to be available. Remember, *everyone gets what they need* in our family. Right now, you need to walk to school with me, because that is safest for you right now. We can reevaluate again in a few months to see if there is a larger group that you can walk with."

Here's one more example: "Charlie, I know you would like to go to a baseball game, but Kyle doesn't like baseball, so it's something we need to do when we can find something else for Kyle to do, because he will be bored and restless and then we won't have fun. Remember, *everyone gets what they need,* and I know you need to go to a baseball game. I'm going to do my best to get you to one as soon as possible, but I can't make Kyle miserable in the process. So be patient, and as soon as we can find someone to watch Kyle for the afternoon, we will get tickets and go."

As you can see, it is most important that your child learns to be flexible and to realize that, in a family, being treated fairly does not always mean being treated the same as one's sibling(s). This is an excellent lesson: throughout life, your child will confront situations where it will be important to feel secure in one's place and to feel empathy for others, rather than jealousy or envy.

7

Money, Money, Money

Your child's interest in money and its importance for purchasing items she wants increases as she moves into the upper elementary grades. For one thing, as her arithmetic skills continue to improve, she learns more and more about how money actually works—the value of paper money compared to coins and the value of higher versus lower denominations of money. It will still be some time before your child truly has a grasp on all the intricacies of saving and spending money, but you will likely begin to see a great leap of understanding in these years.

In this chapter, you will see that your child's questions reflect his greater understanding of money and the complexities that surround the world of purchasing and saving. The way you respond to these questions, and the way you approach giving money to your child and spending money on your child will help him to form his own understanding of the value of money. It will also have a dramatic impact on the way he relates to you about money. For example, every parent wants a child who is appreciative and values the money that is spent on him. *This doesn't happen by accident!* It is directly connected to the way you communicate to your child about money.

We will discuss many issues in this chapter that will help you raise an appreciative, fiscally responsible child. For example—one I am sure will be of great interest to you—we will talk about how to begin giving your child an allowance, which, if done the correct way, will also dramatically increase your child's ability to understand the value of money. This is one of the topics parents ask me about the most wherever I go, so let's begin with the question that relates to it.

#35: CAN I GET MY ALLOWANCE EARLY?
(OR: WILL YOU BUY THIS FOR ME, AND I'LL PAY YOU BACK? CAN I HAVE SOME MONEY? WILL YOU BUY ME...?)

Emily and Claire (both age 10) constantly ask their parents, Sherry and Russell, if they can get their allowances early. Sherry explains, "There's always something they want to buy—a CD, a toy, some junk at the pharmacy. I'm constantly advancing one of them allowance; it's hard to keep track of whom I've given [allowance to] and whom I haven't!"

Allowance is a complex matter in many homes. Parents are not sure at what age to start giving it, how much to give, and what the rules should be for receiving it. Should a child do chores for an allowance or receive it free and clear? Should you give it once a week or less frequently? Can your child lose her allowance for bad behavior? And what about the question here, asked often by elementary-age (and older) kids? Is it okay to advance your child's allowance earlier in the week?

Let's try and sort through all these issues, so you have it straight by the end of this section.

Uncovering the Meaning

ONE: It is best to begin giving your child an allowance when she truly starts to understand the concept of spending and saving money.

The bottom line: For most kids, this is not before six years of age, and for many it is closer to seven or even a bit older. If you do not yet give your child an allowance, don't worry! It is never too late to start.

TWO: You are probably also wondering how much allowance to give your child, right? I bet you have heard the rumor that you are supposed to give $1 for each year of your child's age. Actually, I—and many other professionals—do not subscribe to that theory. For one thing, don't you think that $6 is a lot to give a six-year-old? And for some twelve-year-olds, $12 may not be enough, depending on what they are expected to use their allowances for. Therefore, the amount you give your child should depend on your expectations for how your child will spend the allowance.

For example, if you expect your nine-year-old to use her allowance only for an occasional treat at the drugstore or a pack of gum once in a while, a couple of dollars a week is more than enough. On the other hand, if you want your ten-year-old to spend her money on birthday gifts for friends, some of her clothes, and snacks at the movies, she probably needs closer to $20 a week. This will require her to budget (with your help) for what she wants and is required to purchase.

The bottom line: Your child needs a big enough allowance so that she actually has enough money to spend on the items you expect her to pay for, within a budget, and still be able to save a bit for the future. If you give an allowance that is too small, your child will simply become frustrated, and the meaning of getting an allowance— learning to budget, save, and spend—will be missed.

THREE: Parents frequently tell me that they give their children allowances, but they still ask for Mom or Dad to give them money or buy them things. In fact, the constant nagging to buy, buy, buy is a good signal that your child is ready to receive an allowance. If your child is already receiving one, it means that you are not leveraging it correctly. Keep this in mind: *you* should not *make impulse or unplanned purchases for your child, or purchase items that you do not want to buy that she could buy with her own money.* This is the very reason she receives an allowance. Below, we will discuss what you need to say to your child to help her see that she should use her own money, rather than continuing to ask you to buy her things.

The bottom line: Your child has an allowance so that you don't constantly have to buy things for her. This will only happen if you actually stop purchasing these things.

FOUR: Another big question that I am frequently asked is whether a child's allowance should be tied to chores. The answer is *no*! I know some parents may not like this answer because you would like your child to know that she cannot get money free and clear. Some parents are even tempted to offer their children money (not exactly an allowance) for getting good grades in school. However, there are two reasons that it is important to give an allowance without tying it to anything:

1. A child should be expected to do chores because she is part of a family unit, not because she is being paid to do them. There should be no monetary compensation for it. A child should also be expected to work as hard as possible in school

because this is what is expected of her, by you and by her teachers. This is an integral part of being in a family, and of being a person of pride and integrity. You are not compensated for doing laundry, making beds, cooking dinner, or helping your kids with homework. Yes, you are compensated for working outside of the house, but that is the money on which your family lives. Your child does *not* get paid by school for her hard work! You should not, therefore, foster a sense of entitlement that she should receive compensation for her hard work in school or at home. You should not be afraid to place demands on your child and you do not need to pay her to meet these demands. This is part of raising an emotionally healthy and well-behaved child.

2. The reason you give your child an allowance is to begin teaching her how to use, budget, and save money. When she is older and gets her first job, she will learn about earning money. If you so choose, it is fine to compensate her for doing *extra* chores beyond the regular ones (washing the car, shoveling snow, cleaning the garage, filing, organizing, stuffing envelopes, etc.).

The bottom line: Allowance and chores are to remain separate. Your child's allowance is an experiment in using money; chores are about living in the family.

FIVE: This next issue is actually connected to the previous one—many parents want to know if a child's allowance should be docked for poor behavior. Much as allowance should not be connected to chores, it should also not be related to behavior. As tempting as it is to take away allowance if your child behaves badly, it is more appropriate to give an elementary-age child a consequence that is directly related to the negative behavior, rather than by taking away money. In reality, the docked allowance will not mean nearly as much to her as it means to you. In addition, a consequence that is connected to her behavior—and is immediate—will have a greater impact on her behavior than losing a couple of dollars.

The bottom line: Docking allowance should not be a consequence for negative behavior.

SIX: Some families—like mine—have rules for how a child is allowed to spend her allowance. Even though it is your child's money, I believe that you should still have final veto power. Here are some examples of things you might want to consider within your domain to veto. In our home, allowance cannot be spent on any of these:

- Junk food and soda
- Video/handheld games that have an inappropriate rating
- Inappropriate clothing (too suggestive, negative message written on it, etc.)

Of course, your child will want to spend her money on many other things that you think are a ridiculous waste of money. I know mine do. I do my best to talk them out of these, but never forbid them. Sometimes the lesson of money wasted is well worth it.

The bottom line: Don't be afraid to make rules about how your child spends her money. You're still the parent, and you still make the rules.

SEVEN: Finally! To the question asked by Emily, Claire, and so many other children. Is it okay to advance your child's allowance before she is due to receive it? For the most part, I would suggest that, when your child is in elementary school, it is best not to advance her allowance on a regular basis because it will defeat the purpose of her learning to *wait* and to *save*—two of the main reasons you are giving her an allowance. I speak a great deal about teaching your child *frustration tolerance*—the ability to wait patiently for what she wants, without having a tantrum. I have spoken about frustration tolerance several times throughout the book, so you know that it is an important skill for your child to learn. If you always advance her allowance simply because she asks for it, you take away an excellent opportunity for her to practice frustration tolerance—waiting to purchase something she wants because she can't get it immediately.

Of course, there are exceptions to this rule. If your child rarely asks, and the item she wants will not be available at a later point, you may want to consider lending her the money until she has saved up enough. In this case, it is important to work out a repayment plan and *write it down so she understands it*. It will be difficult for her to remember it—especially after she already has the item she wants—if you don't make it concrete and clear for her. I strongly suggest that you not get in a habit of advancing money in this manner.

Another time when it may be okay to advance money to your child is when she actually has the money at home and she can give it back to you right away. Be clear that you expect her to repay you as soon as she has access to her money, and then make sure that she follows through. The money may be trivial to you, but it is an important lesson for her.

The bottom line: Do not offer an advance on your child's allowance except in rare circumstances, and then be clear that you expect repayment as soon as possible.

The Best Way to Respond

Now that you have a thorough understanding of how to give your elementary-age child an allowance, responding to this question should be simple! Here is an example of a possible response that might work for you: "Sorry, you can't get your allowance early. You will get your allowance on Saturday as usual. If you like, we can go to the store then, and you can buy what you want. If it is not there anymore, you will either find something else or wait until next time. It's probably a good idea to save some of your allowance each week, rather than spending it all, so you have money at the end of the week."

Now I would like to give you a response to help you solve the problem of your child continuing to ask you for money or to buy her things, *despite* the fact that she gets an adequate allowance:

Your child: "Mom, can I have a quarter to get a bouncy ball from the machine in the supermarket?"

You: "Would you spend your own quarter on the machine?"

Your child: "No! It's not worth it."

You: "Right! It's not worth it to spend my money either. Sorry, you can't have a quarter."

Here is another scenario that will help you to realize that when a child must spend his own money, he thinks much harder about whether he really wants something:

Your child: "Can you get me a remote control car?"

You: "You can use your own money."

Your child: "But that's a lot of money!"

You: "Yes, it is. So how come you expect *me* to spend so much of my money? If you want it, you need to save for it. Your birthday is coming up in a month. I'll give you $15 toward it for your birthday, and you need to save the rest."

Your child: "I'll think about it. I don't know if I want it for my birthday. I don't know if I want it *that* much."

The bottom line about allowances: If you want to have a child who truly appreciates the value of your money and her own, you need to make your child's allowance meaningful and valuable. If you buy your child whatever she wants in addition to giving her an allowance, your child will never appreciate or value money or material things—do not expect her to!

- -

#36: HOW MUCH MONEY DO YOU MAKE/DOES DADDY MAKE? (OR: HOW MUCH DID OUR HOUSE/CAR COST?)

- -

Georgia's son Tyler (age 9) asks her lots of personal questions about money, which she is not sure how to answer. She explains, "Tyler is very curious about our finances. He frequently asks me how much money I have in my wallet, how much I earn, how much the check is at a restaurant, and how much various things cost—our house, our car, or a vacation. I'm okay telling him the cost of some things, but not everything. Am I being too secretive?"

It is not at all unusual for a curious child to become interested in the cost of all sorts of items and activities. However, it is also perfectly normal, and in fact advisable, for you to figure out which information you should tell your child and which it is better not to share. Let's explore this topic and figure out the best way to communicate with your child about the cost of your lifestyle in a way that makes him feel included, without revealing more than is appropriate for his age.

Uncovering the Meaning

An elementary-age child is most likely asking this question simply because he wants to gain a frame of reference about how much money grown-ups make when they have jobs. It is also possible that he has participated in or overheard conversations about how much money other people's parents make, so he is curious to compare your income with theirs. At this stage, if you were to tell your child your actual income, he would have little real understanding of how much this means in real life (even if he is the smartest kid on the block!). For example, an eight-year-old doesn't actually understand the real difference in spending power between $50,000, $100,000, and $300,000. Even if you explain it to him, it will mean very little. Even a ten-year-old will not be able to grasp this in a meaningful way. There is therefore no compelling reason to tell your child your actual income.

What's more, your income is likely private family business. Since a young child is not particularly good at keeping secrets, this is not good information to share. While it is fine to ask a child to keep family business private, your child would feel very bad if he accidentally divulged information that you really did not want known. As the adult, it is your responsibility to make sure that you keep it private—particularly since there is no reason that your child needs to know the actual numbers.

In addition to the above reasons, an elementary-age child is not yet ready to understand how you choose to spend your money on big-ticket items. The amounts of money will be overwhelming and confusing to him. Perhaps, by middle or high school, you might begin to share certain larger expenditures with your child, as you think he is able to understand these. When it comes to smaller expenditures, you can decide on a case-by-case basis, depending on your child and on the situation.

The Best Way to Respond

When your child asks about your income, the best response is similar to the following: "I (or we) make enough money to make sure that our family has what we need—food, clothes, and our home. We also have enough for the extras that we *like*—things like the movies, eating out sometimes, and other fun stuff. You don't need to worry about the exact amount of money."

If your child insists on knowing, you might have to add, "That's private grown-up information. When you are a grown-up and you have a job, then you will know how much money you make. But I'm not going to share my money information with you."

When your child asks you the cost of other items, you can decide on an individual basis whether you want to share the information. Here is an example: "It cost our family more than $60 to eat in this restaurant—that's more than $15 for each of the four of us. If you were paying for yourself, it would cost you nearly four weeks allowance because you get $4 a week. That's a lot of money, right?"

NOTE: In the above example, you share the amount, but use it as a valuable lesson, giving your child perspective about the cost of eating out.

And another example: "When you buy a car, you have to pay for the car, for insurance, for gas, and also to fix your car when it needs a repair. It costs hundreds of dollars a month to own a car, thousands of dollars a year—did you know that?"

NOTE: In this example, you do not give your child an exact amount, but you do give a realistic ballpark, so he understands that owning a car is an expensive undertaking.

#37: WHY DO WE HAVE TO GIVE MONEY TO CHARITY?

Douglas was surprised when his daughter Mia (age 7) asked him about giving money to charity. "We talk a lot about helping others, so I thought she understood, but I guess the connection was missed somehow."

Giving money to charity is a difficult concept for elementary-age children. Unless you make it a real part of their everyday lives, it is hard for them to grasp.

Uncovering the Meaning

As your child grows through the elementary years, she is exposed to many new things. If your child goes to a reasonably decent school, one of the things she will be exposed to is doing good deeds, giving to people who are in need, and helping others. It is important to continue to convey this message at home as well. It is especially important to make sure that your child understands the importance of giving money to charity. Sometimes this is taught in school, but not always. Sometimes, at school, the concept of charity is taught through actions and behavior—which are also very important. Teaching your child to give financially is often your job.

One way to do this is to suggest to your child that each week, when she gets her allowance, she should put a small part of it in a piggy bank to give to charity. As a family, you can pick the charity, and you can all save money and donate an amount to it each year. It is usually good to pick a child-centered charity or one that has special significance for your family, because your child (or children) will feel more connected to it.

I often suggest that families pick the charity to which they are going to contribute during the holiday season— so that a child can feel she is giving, not just receiving, gifts. You can change your charity each year if you choose. Then, in addition to (or instead of) weekly allowance money, you can also donate proceeds from bake sales, car washes, or other money collected or earned during the year. This will teach your child the value of giving to charity in a very real way.

The Best Way to Respond

Your response to this question should help your child understand the importance of giving money to charity, not just for the receiver, but also for the giver. A young child also needs to hear a response that includes exactly what the money could be used for, as she probably doesn't truly understand what a very poor person might be missing in her or her family's life. A complete response might be similar to the following: "We give money to charity because it is important to help other people who may not have enough money to buy food. Someone who doesn't have enough money for food might not be able to eat breakfast, lunch, or dinner, or give food to their kids—in fact, they might be hungry all the time. They also might not have money for enough clothes for themselves or for their kids, so they would be cold in the winter, or not have shoes for their feet. They also might not have a home, so they wouldn't have somewhere to live."

#38: ARE THINGS YOU BUY WITH A CREDIT CARD FREE?
(OR: HOW CAN YOU NOT HAVE MONEY IF THERE ARE STILL CHECKS IN THE BOOK?)

Troy (age 8½) couldn't figure out how his mom, Connie, purchased so many things with a little plastic card. Connie had not realized Troy's confusion until he spoke to her about it. "Troy apparently thought that everything I buy with my credit cards is free! I got a good laugh from that. I explained to him that you use the credit card and then you have to pay the bill later, but I'm still not sure that he really gets it."

Buying on credit is a tough concept for kids to understand—even some teenagers still don't get it—especially the part about paying interest. But it is very important for you to begin explaining it to your child when he is in elementary school. Otherwise by the time he is old enough to apply for and receive a credit card—which could be as young as high school, because credit card companies now market heavily to high-school-age kids—he could find himself deep in debt, before you even know about or can stop it.

Uncovering the Meaning

Your elementary-age child is just beginning to gain a good understanding of how money is a powerful agent for purchasing anything and everything. He is learning to save, budget, and spend wisely (thanks to you enforcing a strict policy about how he needs to use his allowance).

But suddenly you tell him that this small piece of plastic works just like money. That does not make very much sense in his mind. How does plastic (or paper, in the case of checks) equal money? In fact, it sounds like it is even better than money, because it seems never to run out! In addition, you can use it to purchase items through the computer—how does that work? Even money can't do that! This little plastic card seems to be very powerful. Your child might be wondering, "Why can't I have one?" In fact, it is not unknown for older children and teens to "borrow" their parents' credit cards to make online purchases without their parents' permission. It is therefore important to include in your explanation about credit cards the rules for their use—including who is allowed to use them.

Your explanation needs to be given at a very simplistic level so that your child can clearly understand what you are saying. This is not the time for a complex description of different types of interest rates or the difference between department store and regular credit cards. The basic information you want to impart is as follows:

- If you use a credit card to buy something, it is like borrowing money. You will need to pay the money back very soon after using it, so you need to make sure you have the actual money.
- You will also have to pay interest—which is the price that you pay for borrowing the money, so you need to have that money ready to pay too. If you don't, the amount you owe gets bigger and bigger.
- It is always better to pay with real money than with a credit card.
- You should *never* use a credit card unless you have a job or your parent says it is okay to have one.

You should *never* apply for a credit card without permission.

- You must *never* borrow a parent's credit card without permission. You will be punished if you do—it is stealing.

The Best Way to Respond

Your elementary-age child needs a clear concrete explanation to really understand the way credit cards work. The same type of explanation is needed to understand the way checks work. It is a good idea to give an example that is directly related to your child's life. For example: "Using a credit card is like borrowing money. When you give the credit card to the person in the store, and he swipes it through the machine, it tells the store that you are borrowing the money from the credit card company and that you are going to pay it back. You always have to pay it back. Like if you borrow money from me to buy a new toy, you have to pay me back the next time you get your allowance. But the credit card company isn't your parent, so it doesn't just lend you the money; it also charge you extra money for letting you borrow it. So let's say I said I would let you borrow $10 for the toy, but I also said you had to pay me an extra $1 because I was letting you borrow the money—that $1 is called interest. You have to pay all that money back, or the credit card company can come and take back the stuff you bought with its money, and even other stuff. So, you should never, ever use a credit card unless you are sure you can pay back the money plus the interest. Some credit card companies let high school kids get cards, but you should never get a credit card when you are a kid unless you have my permission. And you must never borrow my credit card to buy anything from a store or online without my permission. That's like stealing money and you would be punished for doing that. I would know you did it because every month I get a letter from the credit card company telling me everything that is bought with my card."

#39: IF YOU WON'T BUY IT, CAN I ASK GRANDMA?

Suzanne's daughter Anna (age 10) doesn't like to take no for an answer. "If my husband or I tell Anna she can't have something, she immediately asks me if she can ask Grandma or Grandpa if they will buy it for her. I'm conflicted about this. Part of me says, 'Why shouldn't she have it if they don't mind buying it?' but the other part of me says, 'Why can't she just accept that no means no, and she can't always find a way around it?'"

This is a tough call—is Anna being manipulative and stubborn, or is she simply being resourceful? What do you think? Let's explore this question to find out.

Uncovering the Meaning

It is true that a child will often try any means to get what she wants, even if this includes testing all limits and risking angering her parents. In this particular situation, your child is likely asking this question because of one of the following reasons:

In Scenario #1, you have not made clear your *reason* for saying no. Sometimes parents make rules that appear—or are—arbitrary. If you do not take the time to explain your reason for saying no to your child, there is no reason for her to understand your rationale. You may want her simply to accept "because I said so" as a reason to comply, but for many children, this is not motivating enough. We encourage our children to question everything in their world. We can't therefore expect to say no and have them accept it without an explanation. They do not have to be happy with the explanation, or be thrilled that we are saying no, but at least it will make sense to them. Therefore, if your child asks if Grandma can buy her an item that you have denied her, it might be because you have not offered a clear explanation as to why you do not want to buy it.

In Scenario #2, your child knows full well why you are saying no, but she wants to push you as far as she can anyway. Some children are risk-takers. They are even willing to risk being yelled at, reprimanded, or punished on the outside chance that they might get what they want. If your child knows you well, it could be a risk worth taking. For example, if you tend to give in easily, rather than standing firm, your child may be aware that even a gentle nudge will get you to say yes to the suggestion that perhaps her grandparents will buy her what you don't want to purchase. Or perhaps she knows that you will feel guilty having to say no to a big purchase, but that the grandparents will say yes. All she has to do is ask, and you will give in. Or, of course, you might get angry and say no even more forcefully because you made it clear the first time that "no means no," but she's willing to take the risk.

The Best Way to Respond

In Scenario #1 your interchange with your child probably goes as follows:

You: "No, I won't buy you the CD you want."

Your child: "But why?"

You: "Because I said so, that's why!"

Does this sound at all familiar? If it does, then you should know that your child really doesn't understand why you don't want to purchase the CD for her. It seems perfectly logical to her to suggest that perhaps you would allow her to find another person to buy it for her—this would alleviate you of the responsibility, and she would still be able to get what she wants.

It would be better for you to tell her the reason up front, so that it is clear to her. "I am not buying you the CD because it is expensive. You can save your allowance for it if you want to—I'll even pay for half of it if you like, but you'll have to wait until you've saved enough. That's the only way you can get it." If she still wants to know if she can ask Grandma for it, your response should be, "No, we've discussed the way you can get the CD. If you want it, you need to save for it. Grandma buys you lots of things, and you can't ask her for something just because I say no."

In Scenario #2, your exchange with your child might be similar to the following:

You: "I won't buy you that CD because I'm not happy with your behavior today, and you don't deserve a gift."

Your child: "But I'll be behave better now, I promise."

You: "Sorry, no!"

Your child: "Can I ask Grandma to buy it for me then?"

You: "No! Your behavior does not deserve a CD, not from me, Grandma, or anyone else! I hope we are clear. I will talk to Grandma and make sure she doesn't say yes. And if I hear that you asked her, you will have a consequence."

In this scenario, it is important that you make sure that the grandparent (or other parent, baby-sitter, or whomever your child wants to approach) does not undermine your efforts to discipline your child. If such undermining is an ongoing issue, you need to address it directly, because it is not healthy for your child to be able to have that much power.

If you find yourself typically giving in to your child

and allowing her to ask her grandparent (or someone else) for items that you don't want to buy, it is time to rethink this policy. It is okay to disappoint your child. What's more, it is no one else's job to take care of the material needs of your child, unless they do so voluntarily. In fact, you may be placing this person in an awkward position by allowing your child to ask for gifts more frequently than is appropriate. It is also not in your child's best interest.

Remember our old friend, frustration tolerance? Your child needs to learn to wait patiently and to take no for an answer. I promise you, by teaching your child this skill you will have the nicest, most respectful child on the block!

Growing Up
So Fast

With each passing year, the questions your child asks seem to get more and more interesting. However, the questions in *this* chapter are, I believe, some of the toughest ones to answer. Upper-elementary-age children are desperate to grow up and are doing so more and more quickly than ever before. It is *not* your imagination that your child is more sophisticated than you were at the same age. This is fueled partially by the TV shows and movies that children watch. These push children toward being older than they are. This is not only because of the content (see Chapter Three) but also due to the sophisticated manner in which children's media idols dress and behave.

Children are also required to grow up faster because they live in a world that asks them to be more independent. Both parents work, they learn how to use a cell phone (see Chapter One for my view on this), they have busy social lives, and they juggle an array of activities and schoolwork that rivals the amount of work an adult manages—all without a PDA to assist them.

Becoming an independent, busy person at a younger age is not bad for your child. In fact, I think it is great! But it is making her grow up faster. In fact, over the last few years I've noticed that the term "tween" has stretched in its definition. It used to include children in the eleven- and twelve-year-old range. Now most definitions include children beginning at age eight. If you are reading this book, that includes your child. Did you know you already have a tween?

Having a smart, independent child means that you have to be prepared for questions about growing up, independence, bodies, and life, earlier than you might have thought you had to be prepared. So get ready for the ride of your life because once the questions start coming, they won't stop until your child is...well, maybe never! But I'll get you started right now and you'll be ready for them.

#40: WHY CAN'T I STAY HOME ALONE?

Cassidy (age 9) recently started asking her parents if she could stay home alone. Ray and Kelly agree that even though they live in a safe neighborhood, they are not comfortable with this idea. Ray explained, "Cassie gets so annoyed when we tell her we're not comfortable leaving her alone in the house (or with her eight-year-old sister). She'll say, 'Not even for half an hour in the middle of the day?' When I say no, she says, 'You treat me like I'm a baby! I can take care of myself. I know how to dial 911, I know how to cook; you just don't trust me!' I explain that we only let her cook when we are around and that this is different. She insists that she's not a baby."

It always amazes me how differently parents and kids perceive situations—and this discrepancy continues to become wider as your child inches closer to adolescence. The key is to learn how to compromise with your child in a way that maintains her safety but still allows her to feel a sense of autonomy. Once you figure out how to do it now, it will be *much* smoother sailing during the teen years.

Uncovering the Meaning

What is it that empowers your child to want to be so independent at such a young age? For one thing, the media has an enormous influence on your child's desire to experience being alone. TV shows like *iCarly* (Nickelodeon), *Zoey 101* (Nickelodeon), *The Suite Life of Zack and Cody* (Disney Channel), and *Recess* (Disney Channel), which are basically funny and innocuous programs that target elementary-age kids, and depict children and young teens who get into trouble, and then solve their problems with very little adult involvement. If you have never watched them, check out the shows your child is watching, and you'll see what I mean.

Then, of course, there are all the real-life child and teen celebrities who are marketed directly to your school-age child. Not only are they famous, but they appear to be living glamorous and independent lives before reaching adulthood. Consider, for example, famous teens like Miley Cyrus (*Hannah Montana*), the Jonas Brothers, and all the stars of *High School Musical*, to name just a few. It is no wonder your child is asking for a small chance to test out her own skills of independence.

An older sibling, cousin, or even neighborhood friends who are allowed to stay alone may also influence your child's desire to experience the independence of having the house to herself.

So, when is the right age to allow your child to stay home alone? I asked a number of parents. Here is a sampling of their answers:

Brenda: "Twelve is the right age; a child younger than that just isn't ready yet."

Teresa: "I started leaving my son home for an hour or so at ten years old. Our apartment building has a doorman, and a friend lives right next door. He's very mature, and I felt comfortable."

Rodney: "Thirteen or fourteen is young enough. Why rush it? Anything could happen, and you never know if your child could handle it."

Jill: "I have eleven-year-old twins—a girl and a boy. I'd leave my daughter alone but not my son; girls are much more mature and level-headed!"

Colleen: "I haven't left my kids alone yet, and they are ten, twelve, and fourteen. They fight like cats and dogs—I would be afraid of what would happen while I was gone! I keep telling them that when they are mature enough to stop fighting, I'll think about it."

Ron: "When I was growing up, I let myself in to the house after school beginning at age nine. I want my son to do the same, but my wife doesn't agree—she thinks he should be at least eleven."

Tonia: "It depends on your child; some kids are more mature than others, and some are also less afraid to stay alone."

Eva: "It really depends on your neighborhood—if you live somewhere quiet and safe, you can leave your child alone at a younger age than if you live somewhere that is not as safe."

As you can see, there is definitely no *one* right or wrong answer! In fact, only two states officially regulate the age at which a child is not permitted to be left alone: Maryland (under eight years) and Illinois (under fourteen years). In every other state, it is left to the discretion of a parent, although some states offer strong guidelines. In addition, many local communities may have regulations as to an age at which it is acceptable to leave a child alone. If you are not sure how to learn about such guidelines, you should call your local Child Protective Services office. If you are not sure how to reach your local office, you can call Childhelp USA (www.childhelp.org) at (800) 4-A-CHILD (422-4453). They will be able to help you find the contact information for your local office.

Aside from possible regulations or guidelines, there are multiple other factors to consider when thinking about whether your child is ready to be left alone (in addition to her asking you over and over again). To begin, I recommend that, at an absolute minimum, any child under ten is too young to be left alone, no matter how much she begs (notwithstanding Maryland's law). Even a mature eight- or nine-year-old does not have the cognitive ability, judgment, or emotional maturity to handle the possible problems, crises, or temptations of being alone at home.

Once you have established this bottom line, you need to feel comfortable with your child's level of maturity. Can you answer yes to all of the following questions?

- Does your child follow directions and rules?
- Does your child typically use good judgment, rather than being someone who engages in dangerous, impulsive, or risky behavior?
- Is your child usually truthful? Do your trust her?
- Can your child make an emergency phone call with confidence? If necessary, you should role-play to find out.

- Is your child generally responsible about important aspects of her life (homework, chores, etc.)?
- Does your child stay calm in the face of something unexpected (the doorbell rings, she must talk to a stranger on the phone, she gets a small cut, the smoke alarm goes off, there's a power outage)?

If you can comfortably respond yes to all of the above—including all aspects of the last point—your child may be ready to stay home alone, as long as you are ready for her to do so. Your comfort level may depend on the area in which you live as well as your own life experience. However, be careful not to let your own anxiety get in the way if all other factors point in the direction of giving your child a chance.

The Best Way to Respond

If your child is under ten, or younger than the age at which you feel comfortable leaving her home alone, a clear answer will be best—for both of you. Saying, "We'll see" or "I'll think about it" will only make her keep asking, increasing both your and her frustration. A response similar to the following may not make her happy, but at least she will know where you stand: "Cassie, nine is too young to stay home alone. In fact, I am not going to be comfortable leaving you home by yourself until you are at least eleven. We will discuss it again then. It doesn't matter to me what other families do; this is *our* rule in *our* family. I can't even promise you that I will be comfortable when you are eleven, but I definitely won't be before that. I can promise that if you keep nagging me, it will make me angry, and then eleven won't even be looking so good!"

Once you decide that you are ready to let your child stay home alone, it is best to do so for a short while (half an hour to an hour) for the first couple of times, to see how it goes. In addition, your child needs to know the following:

- How to reach you and at least one other close relative or friend, in addition to knowing how to call 911 and communicate her full name, address, and phone number.
- When you or another adult is expected home (if your plans change, call your child).
- Not to open the door to anyone—even someone she knows—except with express permission from you.
- To never tell a phone caller that there is no adult at home. Teach your child either to say you are busy or to screen calls.
- Not to touch the stove, toaster, microwave, hair dryer, curling iron, space-heater, or any other heated appliances without your specific permission.
- To leave immediately if there is a fire—even a small one.
- That friends are not allowed to come over without your permission.

- If your child arrives home to an empty house, to routinely check in with you or another adult. She should not enter if the door is already open or if a window is broken, and she should leave if anything looks suspicious upon entering.
- The rules: when to do homework; how much TV/computer/electronics are allowed, what she is allowed to eat, chores she is expected to do.
- How to turn off your home security system and what to do if it accidentally goes off (do you have a code that she will have to tell to a dispatcher?).

Once you are ready to leave your child alone, you too have responsibilities:

- Secure all medications (other than those with which you trust your child, such as a child's dose of painkiller).
- Lock up cigarettes, matches, lighters, car keys, and alcohol. If you own a firearm, that too *must* be dismantled and locked up separately from ammunition.
- Keep flashlights handy and working in case of a power outage, and make sure your child knows where they are.
- Keep your home stocked with healthy food, not junk food.
- Role-play with your child—the more practice she gets, the more likely it is that she will be able to handle a real emergency situation.

#41: WHEN AM I GOING TO GET HAIR UNDER MY ARMS/GROW BREASTS/ NEED TO SHAVE?

Justin (age 10) has an older brother whom he watches very carefully. Justin's mother, Jen, told me that he frequently asks her questions about his body. "Justin asks me all kinds of questions about when his body will change, but he is mostly interested in hair. He regularly asks me when he will get pubic hair. I can't tell if he wants it or if he's nervous to get it."

It is probably a little bit of both! Many children anticipate puberty with a combination of fear, anxiety, and a bit of excitement. In many cases, a child takes his cues from his parent, so it is important to approach his questions in a way that will make him feel positive rather than negative about the upcoming changes—especially since he doesn't have any choice about them.

Uncovering the Meaning

Questions from an elementary-age child about puberty usually arises as the result of a child observing changes in a sibling or peer's body, because of conversations among peers or following educational programming in school that addresses puberty. Sometimes a child will start asking questions after reading about it—perhaps he found a book you gave to an older sibling who was approaching puberty. In some cases, a child is beginning to experience changes in his own body.

Some children will show early interest in learning about puberty, while others will show very little interest until they are older. Similarly, children's bodies also change at different rates.

Girls usually begin to show puberty changes anywhere between eight and thirteen years old. The first change is usually the development of breast buds, which are hard lumps under each nipple. They may hurt a bit to the touch, and they may not be completely even (which could upset your daughter). Pubic and then underarm hair are usually the next to develop (although they could be first). Over the next year or two, her breasts will continue growing and her pubic hair will change, becoming coarser, and her body, hands, and feet will also grow. Menstruation is usually the last change to occur, often arriving approximately a year after the beginning of puberty.

Boys typically don't enter puberty until they are eleven or twelve years old. The first signs are testicle and penis growth, and then the appearance of pubic and underarm hair. Boys will also have at least one growth spurt during adolescence (yes—that is when you are buying new clothes and shoes every three months!). Boys will also experience deepening of their voices—some, but not all, will experience "cracking" as their voice changes to a more adult voice.

While they move through puberty, both boys and girls can experience pimples, acne, greasy skin and hair, weight gain, as well as awkwardness with their bodies. This is a normal, albeit somewhat stressful part of growing up.

Talking to your child about puberty is important. In fact, the more relaxed and calm you are about talking to your child, the less awkward both you and he will feel. Do not assume that your child's school is going to do the job for you. While some school-based programs are excellent, this is not always the case. Poorly trained consultants run some. In other situations, reluctant school staff is forced to run the program. For example, an uncomfortable gym teacher may feel stressed out talking about puberty, but will do it if he doesn't have a choice. It is unlikely that the children in his puberty program will leave the program feeling less anxious or less curious. In fact, the teacher's anxiety may make them feel more nervous. Your child is likely to come home that day with lots of questions.

The Best Way to Respond

The best way to respond to your child's puberty questions is to begin by being as factual and concrete as possible and for you to be relaxed. Using the information above, explain to your child how puberty works. Understanding the facts will make him less nervous. Of course, you can't give him an exact time line, unless you already see signs of development (which is more likely if you have a daughter). However, you can offer an estimate for when changes will occur. Make sure he understands that it is different for everyone and that it is normal to be wondering about it.

It is also important to use the real names of body parts and encourage him to do the same. This will signal to your child that you are comfortable with the topic and that you don't need to hide behind silly or babyish names. If you have a hard time saying *penis*, *testicles*, *vagina*, *breasts*, or any other words you may need for your discussion, try saying them to yourself aloud or to another adult until you feel comfortable with them.

Ask your child lots of questions along the way, to be sure that your child understands what you are explaining. An example of a response might be similar to the following: "Growing hair under your arms is probably about the second or third part of puberty for a boy. Do you know what puberty is? It is when your body starts to change—when you start to go from being a kid to being more grown-up. You might notice your testicles and your penis getting bigger. You also might start to notice hair growing around your penis and then under your arms. All of that will probably start when you are anywhere from eleven years old and up. It is different for every kid. You are normal if it starts when you are eleven, and you're also normal if it doesn't start until you're thirteen. Do you understand?"

If you find it awkward to have frank discussions about puberty, there is no shame in giving your child a book. However, I strongly suggest that you read the book *with* your child, rather than simply giving it to him and letting him read it alone. It is important to have as much open conversation as possible. You should use the book as a springboard to begin conversation, rather than communicating to your child that the book is meant *in place of a conversation.*

#42: AM I FAT?

"Shelby (age 9) seems too young to be asking about her weight!" worries her mother, Lesley. "I'd expect it from my thirteen-year-old daughter, but not at nine! It really upsets me."

Lesley's concern is understandable. After all, Shelby does seem too young to be experiencing body image pressures and worries of whether or not she is happy with her body. However, more and more girls these days are concerned about their bodies and weight at younger ages. Given the problems with both being overweight and with eating disorders among both girls *and* boys, this is an important issue. So, what does this question mean, and how should you handle it?

Uncovering the Meaning

There are many factors that contribute to a child asking this question at such a young age. The most obvious reason is that perhaps your child really is overweight and she has been teased about this in school. Clearly, teasing is *never* acceptable. However, if your child is overweight and she has been teased, this question certainly makes sense.

For girls, early puberty can also trigger feelings of being fat—especially compared to other girls who have not yet entered puberty. Unfortunately, teasing and peer pressure begin at a young age. For both boys and girls, teasing and comparing bodies can begin as young as third grade.

A child may also become concerned about her weight due to a steady diet of media that exposes her to very, very thin actresses and actors. When she becomes enamored with the super-skinny stars of TV shows and movies, it is difficult for her to keep perspective about what a healthy body really looks like. She begins to doubt her own body. Boys too experience this pressure because many of their media role models are tall, thin, and muscular—something that most elementary-age boys won't be for a long time (if ever). This self-doubt is further increased by many of the fashions that are created for kids—both boys and girls. Most styles are cut so slim that even an average-size child feels fat when trying them on.

You may not have to look as far as your TV set to find pressure that could be negatively influencing your child's body image. It is possible that without even realizing it, you are communicating negative messages to your child that are making her feel bad about her body. Answer the following four questions honestly:

1. Do you criticize your own body in front of your child ("I hate my thighs," "I'm so fat," etc.) or weigh yourself frequently?

2. Do you take eating healthy food to an extreme (eating salad and "diet" food, drinking diet soda, skipping meals)? You may need someone else's feedback to answer this question accurately.

3. Do you spend more time exercising and talking about exercise than just about anything else?

4. Do you talk to your friends (in person and on the phone), in your child's presence, about other people's bodies ("She's so fat," "I can't believe she gained so much weight")?

If you answered yes to one or more of these questions, you could, inadvertently, be communicating disapproval to your child about her body. If your child knows that you don't like your body, she will assume that she is not supposed to like hers—you are role-modeling that for her. If you overdo the healthy eating and/or exercise, she will feel inadequate compared to you, which will make her think that she's fat—or wonder if you think she is fat.

Last, if you talk critically about other people, she is sure to wonder if you are talking about her behind her back. In addition, you are teaching your child to be a gossip.

The Best Way to Respond

If your child really is overweight, you will want to resist the urge to focus the conversation on the child who made the comment. Acknowledge that it may have hurt your child's feelings, but then use this as an opportunity to talk to your child about what she—and your whole family—can do to make changes toward a healthier lifestyle. Your conversation may be similar to the following: "I'm sure it hurt your feelings to have someone call you fat—that's not a nice thing to say. However, maybe it is time for us to talk a little about your weight, because I have a feeling that it bothers you too. So, we are going to start making some healthy changes in our family to help all of us become healthier. We'll exercise more and eat more healthily. Then maybe you will start to feel better about your body."

If you need an extra boost to help your child on the road to a healthier body, check out my book *Dr. Susan's Fit and Fun Family Action Plan* to get you going with some great solutions for a healthier family.

When a child's concern is related to puberty changes, reassurance is the best strategy. Explain that everyone's body changes and that it doesn't mean she is fat.

In addition, no matter what the reason, give her some

language to use in case of teasing or peer pressure. You should practice saying the following phrases with your child—boys and girls. Even if your child doesn't have enough courage to use them with another child, simply saying them to herself will help her develop stronger self-esteem and a better body image. Of course, using them when teased or pressured is the ultimate goal. For example, try these phrases:

- "It is mean to hurt other people's feelings."
- "I'm not fat; all bodies look different."
- "You're not nice, that's why you're saying rude things to me. It has nothing to do with me!"
- "I'm happy the way I am; I don't want to look exactly like everyone else."
- "I'm healthy, and I take care of my body. Being too skinny isn't good for you because you need to eat enough."

If you believe your child's question is the result of subtle messages that you are communicating with your own behavior, you probably realize how important it will be for you to change these behaviors. Simply review the questions to which you answered yes in the prior section. You will need to change your behaviors so that the messages you are now sending your child include a strong, healthy body image and a healthier relationship with food and exercise. For example, you may need to hide the scale and stop the negative self-talk. Perhaps you should start eating more well-balanced meals that include more than diet food (this does not mean eating junk food). Include protein, complex carbs, fruit, and veggies, as well as healthy snacks. Your child needs to see that you *eat*—not that you starve yourself. In addition, exercise is important, but too much exercise will overstress your body and will communicate to your child that you prioritize this over anything else. When you are finished exercising, change into different clothes, so your child can see that you have other interests in your life.

- -

#43: HOW DOES A BABY GET OUT OF THE MOMMY'S TUMMY?
(OR: DOES THE DOCTOR TAKE THE BABY OUT? DOES THE BABY COME OUT OF THE MOMMY'S BELLY BUTTON? I KNOW HOW BABIES GET IN, BUT HOW DO THEY GET OUT?)

- -

Antonio (age 8) seemed shocked after asking his pregnant mother, Yvette, how the baby would get out of her tummy. "I explained to him that the baby would come out of my vagina. 'That is so weird and gross,' he said. 'I didn't know it came from there!'"

Younger kids are satisfied with simple answers to the more typical question "where do babies come from?" as I explained in *The Top 50 Questions Kids Ask*

(Pre-K through 2nd Grade). But your older child often asks much more sophisticated questions about this topic that typically require more complex responses—responses that may make you squirm if you don't feel equipped to answer them properly. So read this section carefully, and you won't be stuck for the right answer to a tough question.

Uncovering the Meaning

There are many reasons your child is asking questions that are more detailed, about babies and probably about almost everything. To begin, his brain is growing in leaps and bounds. Extensive learning in school is fueling this cognitive growth. Your child is being taught to ask lots of questions—by his classroom teacher, by his science teacher, and by all the other wonderful educators in his life. So this is exactly what he is doing.

He may also be hearing a lot from other children on the playground, on the school bus, and in school. Children share information with each other, but this doesn't mean that they share accurate information. It is therefore important that beginning now, at this young age, you have open and frank conversations with your child about topics that may make you feel awkward, but about which he is curious.

If he doesn't get accurate information from you, he will continue to believe the misinformation he is receiving from other sources. Today it is about how babies are born—tomorrow it could be about drugs and sex. Opening the door of communication now—and keeping it open—is vitally important in your relationship with your child.

You therefore need to take the plunge and answer the tough questions. Your child is no longer satisfied with a simplistic response, as he might have been just a year or two ago. Now, each answer you give is probably followed by another question. He wants details! On the other hand, this does not mean that you have to give him every single detail. Rather, you need to ensure that you are giving your child enough information to satisfy most of his curiosity, but not so much that it will frighten or overstimulate him.

The Best Way to Respond

For example, it is appropriate and important to tell your child—as Yvette did—that a baby is usually born from a mother's vagina. You can explain that the vagina is similar to a rubber band because it can stretch so the baby can come out, and then it returns to its regular shape again. Your child may find this explanation "gross" or "weird" at first, but he will get used to it. You can also add that sometimes the doctor takes the baby out of the mommy's tummy—but not through the belly button (as many children think).

His next question will likely be, "Does it hurt?" While honesty is important, I would suggest that you not focus on this aspect of the process. It is not necessary for a child—especially a girl—to carry around the worry that childbirth is painful. There is plenty of time in the future to have to confront this concern. A satisfying response that wouldn't alarm your child could be, "It might hurt a bit, but it's worth it to have a beautiful baby."

#44: WHAT DOES *GAY* MEAN?

Carl and Darlene admitted that they weren't sure how to respond when their daughter Jasmine (age 10) asked them this question. Carl explained, "Jasmine said that she heard one of the kids on the bus saying to another kid, 'You're so gay!' She asked us what it meant. I bet the kids didn't even know themselves—they just thought it was some kind of an insult. But we weren't sure if we should give her a full explanation and explain why it isn't nice to use that as an insult, or if she's too young and we should just tell her it isn't a nice thing to say to someone."

Parents are often not sure when and how to explain "being gay" to a child. However, since it is a term that is frequently used among older-elementary-age kids, it is important to become comfortable with knowing when it is the right time to answer this question or a similar one.

Uncovering the Meaning

Many children hear the word "gay" for the first time, just as Jasmine did, thrown around as a vague insult among children—having little to do with its actual meaning, because even the kids using it don't know what they're saying. The kids saying it, as well as those hearing it, typically assume it means something like, "You're so lame," "You're such an idiot," or a similar mildly derogatory term.

In other instances, your child might hear the word for the first time in a more serious setting. For example, perhaps she has recently overheard a conversation about a person who is gay, or maybe she knows someone who is gay, but doesn't actually know what the word means.

Sometimes children—who can be very astute—sense that this is an "unusual" word, connected to a topic that makes some adults uncomfortable. Therefore, your child may not ask you the meaning of the word "gay" if she senses that you are an adult who is not comfortable with the concept of homosexuality. For example, your child may have asked you about the word before or brought it up in your presence. However, if you have ignored it or changed the subject, this is a cue to your child that it is not a subject with which you are comfortable. So don't be surprised if your child is reluctant to discuss it with you again.

Of course, much like the previous question, it is important to be as open as possible with your child about all subjects, because as your child grows up, you want her to feel that she can approach you with questions about any subject—no matter how awkward or seemingly "taboo." It is therefore well worth it for you to work toward overcoming your own feelings of embarrassment or awkwardness about this topic, so you can talk to your child about it openly. Remember, *not* talking about it will not make her questions go away; she will simply seek answers elsewhere—answers that may not be accurate.

The Best Way to Respond

The best way to respond to this question is to be as simple and clear as possible. In addition, give your child a response that dispels any possibility that she will use the word "gay" in a derogatory manner, and also help her recognize when others are doing so. Remember that your child does not have any preconceived notions about homosexuality. Even if you have the urge to do so, this is not the time to place judgment or to tell your child that you don't agree with being gay; it is also not the time for a religious conversation about homosexuality or about whether people choose or don't choose to be gay. This will all be confusing and does not answer her question. Your goal is to keep the explanation as simple as possible In other words, do your best to keep *your* agenda separate from *her* agenda!

A great response might be similar to the following: "Most grown-ups you know have a husband or a wife, a girlfriend or a boyfriend. Men date and marry women; girls go out with boys. Sometimes, though, men are attracted to other men, or women are attracted to other women—that is called "being gay." A man may even fall in love with another man, or a woman with another woman. A different word that means the same as *gay* is *homosexual*. There are all kinds of love in the world—this is one kind of love. It is not okay to tease or make fun of people who are gay—just as you wouldn't make fun of anyone else who is different from you. It is *also* not okay to use the word *gay* to tease or make fun of other people, as if being gay is a bad thing. For example, I never want to hear you saying, 'That's so gay,' or 'You're so gay.' If you hear someone else saying it, you either need to tell them to stop or you should ignore them. But either way, you shouldn't do it yourself. It's always important to respect other people, and we do that by the way we behave."

#45: WHAT SHOULD I BE WHEN I GROW UP?

"Parker (age 9½) and Jeremy (age 7½) are always asking me what they should be when they grow up," explained the boys' mother, Bonnie. "Parker always says that he wants to be an engineer like his dad, and Jeremy—the shortest kid in the class—tells me he wants to be an

NBA basketball player. How much should I be guiding them at this point? I don't want to stifle their dreams, but I don't want them to be unrealistic either."

This is a very common question. In fact, you might be surprised to know that a child begins to wonder about his future beginning as early as five or six years old. In fact, I address it in *The Top 50 Questions Kids Ask (Pre-K through 2nd Grade)*. If you have a younger child, you will be surprised to see the developmental difference between the two age groups.

The way you respond to this question can help your child begin exploring all the possibilities for his future and, at the same time, do so realistically and with confidence.

Uncovering the Meaning

It is not unusual for an elementary-age child to decide that when he grows up, he wants to do whatever his parent does—sometimes the parent of the same gender, but not always, particularly if one parent does not hold a position outside the home. The reasons for this are fairly simple. First, a parent's job or profession is the one with which he is most familiar. The second reason involves a little psychology (you know I am always slipping it in!). Your child may, at a young age, decide that he wants to do whatever you do (or what his other parent does) because he is subconsciously concerned that, if he doesn't, you will feel rejected and become upset or angry with him.

Of course, it is possible that this subconscious feeling resides completely within your child. However, sometimes, without even realizing it, a parent places expectations on a child to take over a family business, or to become a doctor, a lawyer, an engineer, or a police officer. Even prior to all of that, sometimes a parent inadvertently give a child a subtle message that she expects him to attend a certain level of college or even a specific college—perhaps one that the parent attended. Hannah (age 10), with whom I have worked for quite a while, told me the following: "My parents have dressed me in University of Pennsylvania clothes since I was born—I've seen the baby pictures! It's where they met. Sweatshirts, T-shirts, sweatpants, everything! They haven't exactly told me they want me to go to college there, but it's obvious. But what if I can't get in—isn't it a really hard school to get into?"

Beginning at a young age, children like Hannah often feel a great deal of pressure to meet the unspoken expectations of their parents to choose a specific path when they grow up. In addition, sometimes the path taken by an older sibling can have an impact on the choices that a child makes, unless a parent helps him to forge his own way. For example, if a child has an older sibling with a scientific mind who heads along the path of becoming premed, and then receives a lot of positive attention for doing so, a younger child may force himself along this same path, even if it is not his calling. This questioning of future identity can begin at a very young age, not because a child really knows what he wants to do, but because he wants to receive positive attention and approval from his parents.

What if your child is more like Jeremy—a dreamer whose career goal, in the real world, seems wholly unreachable? Should you step in and give him a reality check, or just let it be for now? It is not unusual for elementary-age children to foster fabulous dreams of the future. In fact, even middle-school-age children still hold onto fantasies that may not come true. But what if they do? Now is not the time to destroy your child's dreams. There will be plenty of time for reality later on in life. However, if your child wants to be a basketball player, a pianist, a figure skater, or any other wonderful fantasy—there is nothing wrong with reminding him that, in order to have any hope of achieving this dream, he will have to practice a lot. Commitment to any activity offers excellent discipline for your child.

The Best Way to Respond

We just covered a lot of information, so when your child asks you this question, it is vital that you think about all of it before you respond. To help you, there are three easy rules to follow when answering this question:

1. Tell your child that he can be anything that he wants to be, as long as he loves it and he makes enough money to support himself.

2. Tell him that he doesn't have to do what you do or what his other parent does—you won't be upset or disappointed (this rule also applies to attending college, as discussed earlier).

3. Explain that he won't have to decide what he wants to do until he is much older, so for now he should enjoy having fun and trying out different things he likes to do. He can also change his mind as many times as he wants.

You may need to answer this question several times more as your child grows up. In every case, be aware that you should not make your child feel that your dreams need to be his accomplishments. Allow him to explore, to experiment, and to discover his own strengths and interests along the way. As difficult as it may be for you, he may not attend the college you wish for (he may not want to or have the ability), and he may not choose the career path you hope he will. In fact, as your child grows up and eventually becomes an adult, there will be many times in life when you don't see eye to eye. Offer guidance and support. Insist on hard work, integrity, and honesty. At the same time, allow for and celebrate individuality and creativity in all areas of life.

9

Just between You and Me

The older elementary years bring about change in so many different ways for your child. Aside from exciting social and cognitive shifts, she also begins to think more about her relationship with you. After all, despite the fact that she is becoming more social, you are still the most important person in her life. It is not until the early adolescent years that your child's peers will truly become the center of her universe.

Your child's new cognitive maturity allows him to begin thinking beyond his everyday world. He is developing empathy and interest in the lives of others, including a fascination with aspects of your life. In addition, his greater understanding of the sequence of time piques his curiosity about the past, and about the future. His questions reflect these developmental and cognitive changes.

Parents (and even teachers) are often surprised—and are sometimes even dumbfounded—by the amazing questions kids ask (I know I am!). Yet, it pays to be prepared for the curve balls, because that is usually when a child *most* needs you to be ready with a clear and supportive response. So, before we tackle the questions, here are a few tips for how to handle any tough, challenging, or surprising personal questions your child throws at you:

- Buy some time to collect your thoughts by answering a question with a question (you know, my favorite psychological technique!).

- It is okay if you don't know the answer—in fact, it helps your child see that it is fine to not know all the answers. If this happens, respond by saying, "You know, I don't know, but I'll find out and get back to you as soon as I know the answer." Then find out ASAP, and report back.

- Some questions have answers that are not appropriate for a young child to know (for example, the details of a murder), or that you feel are too personal (for example, the details of your sex life). In these instances, it is fine not to answer the question. You might say, "You are too young to know the answer to that question. I'll tell you when you are older," or "That's private, so I'm not going to tell you the answer." Do not cave to nagging or tantrums.

- Remember that your child's questions about body parts, puberty, sex, or similar intimate topics simply reflect curiosity. Embarrassment is an adult emotion, so do your best to keep it out of your responses. When you project embarrassment in a conversation, your child will *become* embarrassed because you are cuing him to feel this way.
- Sometimes honesty is the best policy, but not always. Responding in a way that reflects what is emotionally best for your child *is always* the best policy.

Now that we have established the parameters for facing tough questions head-on, it is time to tackle the questions. Remember, when you respond to your child's questions about your life, and about the past and the future in an open and interested way, you will encourage a positive and genuine relationship between your and your child. You will then carry this relationship through your child's early years and into adolescence and adulthood.

#46: DID YOU SMOKE/DRINK/USE DRUGS?

Gary thought his son Tristan (age 11) would be a teenager before he had to confront the *big* questions. "Tristan and I were watching TV when an ad came on about parents talking to kids about drugs. He turned to me and asked, 'Dad, did you ever use drugs?' I was completely taken by surprise!"

Like Gary, many parents believe an elementary-age child will not ask this question. However, many do, and they expect an answer! So don't be taken by surprise and find yourself unprepared to respond.

Uncovering the Meaning

Effective and powerful TV campaigns against drugs, alcohol, and tobacco use are one of the primary reasons that children learn about these taboos at a young age, even if they don't hear about them in other places until they are older. In fact, if your child has not yet asked you about drugs, alcohol, or cigarettes, it could be just around the corner! Seeing ads on TV creates a heightened awareness about illegal substances, which causes older-elementary-age children to become curious.

In addition, some elementary school curricula do begin discussing these topics—especially the dangers of smoking. Further, if you have an older child, your younger one is even more likely to become aware of the topic through conversations you may have with your older child. Even if you don't have an older child, many children mingle with older cousins and other older children on the school or summer-camp bus, and in various other situations. They very frequently overhear conversations about alcohol, drugs, and tobacco. You may also have had an older relative who died from a smoking-related death about which you have told your child, because you want him to understand the dangers of smoking cigarettes.

You can't protect your child forever. He will begin wondering, and the questions will come next. It could be much later—but it could be right now.

Parents who did not smoke cigarettes, drink alcohol, or use drugs as teens don't fret about responding to this question—they can simply be honest in their responses. However, if you are one of the many, *many* parents that did experiment as a teen, I am sure you worry greatly about what to say to your child—especially a young child.

Therefore, you might be surprised to learn that when a young child asks this question, it is not with the same "ulterior motive" that a teen might have. Your elementary-age child is not hoping that you will say yes, so he can then use your response as leverage, an excuse, or a reason to make it okay to experiment himself—this is the reasoning of a much older child.

Developmentally, your young child is—through media, school, and your conversations—being indoctrinated to believe that smoking, drinking, and using drugs are very bad, dangerous, and scary. He is frightened by the thought that kids use them. In fact, when a younger child hears that a teen sibling was "caught" drinking or smoking, he often becomes distraught—not because his brother or sister will get in trouble, but that he or she might be badly injured or killed from exposure to the cigarettes, alcohol, or drugs.

(Needless to say, for the vast majority of children, this feeling does not last beyond the mid- to late-teen years, which is when many kids begin experimenting with alcohol and potentially marijuana or other drugs. Some also try tobacco at this time—and subsequently become addicted.)

Therefore, when your child asks you this question (even a child at the older end of this age range), he is curious and also probably a bit scared that you might say that when you were a teen you did something as bad, dangerous, and scary as drinking, smoking, or using drugs.

The Best Way to Respond

In responding to your child, it is important to keep in mind that your agenda is not exactly the same as it would be if a teen asked you the same question. To begin, remember that your child is fearful during this developmental stage. What's more, he is probably not facing peer pressure, not feeling an internal drive to try illegal substances, and he probably doesn't even have the opportunity.

Nevertheless, you still want to communicate some of the same information that you would share with an older child. To begin, it is critical that you communicate your strong disapproval of your child ever using drugs. Research consistently shows that *the clearer a parent is in voicing his or her disapproval about a child's potential tobacco, alcohol, or drug use, the less likely the child is to try it.* Despite what many parents imagine, "What would my parents think?" is a critical part of a child or teen's decision-making process and a significant deterrent when it comes to experimentation. You need to begin communicating this message in the elementary years, as soon as your child shows an interest in the topic.

So how do you respond to this question? To begin, it is not a great idea to lie, no matter how tempting. There is always the chance that your child may discover your lie later on, which could damage your relationship with him. Rather, while giving your child as little information as possible (remember, you are *not* talking to a teen), you should tell your child the truth. Follow this with a clear and strong message that you forbid him from ever trying tobacco, alcohol, or drugs. In addition, your response should include information that is helpful in building your child's self-confidence and resistance to peer pressure. It is beneficial to use an analogy in your child's current life, so that he understands what you are explaining in a concrete way.

Keep in mind that you may have to have similar conversations many more times and that these conversations may change as your child gets older.

Your response might be similar to the following: "When I was a teenager, I tried alcohol. I knew it was the wrong thing to do because my parents had told me never to do it. I felt really, really guilty afterward because I knew that I was doing something I wasn't supposed to do. Also, it tasted really disgusting. I realized that I should have done the right thing rather than listening to my friends. Remember when William said to you, 'Come on, let's make fun of that weird kid,' and you said, 'No, that's mean, and he's not weird.' Well, I should have stood up to my friends like that and said "No, I'm not trying alcohol; it's not right! I'm going to listen to my parents.' But, Tristan, you are *never* allowed to try alcohol, cigarettes, or any kind of drugs— not ever, even when you're a teenager. I would be very angry, and you will get a very big punishment if I ever catch you—and I will catch you! We know a lot more about how dangerous they all are than we did when I was a kid. They really hurt kids' brains and can even kill you!"

It is important that you have a clear understanding yourself and that you articulate to your child that, no matter what you may have done, you are now concerned about your child's future. Your past is not actually relevant. We know much more about the dangers of tobacco than we ever did. In addition, alcohol is a gateway to marijuana and to other dangerous drugs, all of which are much more powerful and dangerous—even more lethal—than they were when you were a teen. For further information about how to communicate with children and teens about alcohol, cigarettes, and drugs, I highly recommend www.theantidrug.com, a website for parents that clearly addresses just about every issue that they may need to know.

#47: WHY DID YOU MARRY DAD/MOM?

"Grace (age 8) is curious about everything," remarked her mom, Rhonda. "But I was really stumped when she asked me why I married her dad. You see, we're getting divorced, and I wasn't sure exactly how to respond to this question."

That certainly is a curve ball for Rhonda. In fact, there are many different reasons that your child might ask you this question. Let's explore these so you are more prepared than she was, and also so that you get a little peek into the inner workings of your child's mind, in order to comprehend what she is trying to learn about and understand as she grows up.

Uncovering the Meaning

We will begin with some of the straightforward reasons your child might ask you this question. One of the most common reasons is because she is simply curious about the mechanism of how marriage works. Perhaps she has been asked to be a flower girl in a wedding, or maybe a teacher is getting married. This prompts her to think beyond the actual event to consider the relationships involved. This is a good sign! It means your child is developing more advanced cognitive and social skills. She is curious about relationships—what exactly is involved: the feelings, the love, the progression of a relationship, the long-term commitment to each other. In this age-range, girls are more likely than boys to show this level of interest in relationships. Boys are still more fascinated with playing sports and games than they are in the intricacies of relationships. This is not a sexist comment; it is simply factual. Of course, this is not true of *every* boy (remember, there are ranges for all areas of development), but it is a strong norm. If you're not sure that this is what your child is wondering about, exploratory questions will help you figure it out.

Your child's question may also be prompted by worry. Perhaps there is a lot of arguing in your home, and she is concerned about your relationship with her other parent. Is it stable? Might you break up? She may be asking you the question as a way to open up the conversation so she can ask you why you argue so much or to suggest to you that you married for love, so why are you fighting? Children often perceive adult arguing as much worse than it actually is, so your child might be anxious about this, even if your relationship is secure. However, perhaps you need to consider that you are arguing too much in front of your child (or within her hearing).

If you frequently say negative things about your child's other parent, complain about him, or put him down in front of your child, it could also prompt the question. Your child might begin to wonder why you married someone whom you don't like, or about whom you are always complaining. Is this the way you want your child to perceive her other parent? I hope the answer is no! In which case, you need to immediately become aware of your behavior and change it.

However, if you intentionally (even subconsciously) want your child to perceive her other parent negatively, we have a much bigger problem, because it means you are allowing *your* negative feelings to interfere with what is best for your child. It is *never* in a child's best interest to have one parent speak negatively about the other parent. In fact, it is emotionally destructive. If this sounds like your family, and you're not sure that you can work it out yourself, perhaps you need to seek professional help from a child or family psychologist or other mental health counselor trained to work with families so that your child's emotional health isn't further jeopardized.

Last, maybe your child is asking this question for the same reason as Grace—to try to understand a divorce or separation. It is hard for a child to understand how her parents could have been so in love, then gotten married and had a child (or more than one), and then fallen so far out of love that they now want nothing more to do with each other. For a child in this situation, wanting to understand why her parents were married in the first place is an important question to have answered, not only for now, but so she can understand what not to do herself in the future. (In fact, it is probably an important question to answer for yourself, so you do not repeat the same mistakes again—but I digress.)

The Best Way to Respond

Clearly, the way you respond to your child's question depends on the reason she is asking it. It is therefore important that you take the time to explore her question by chatting with her about it, before offering a definitive answer. *Answering her question with a question* is the first thing to do. An example of a possible dialogue might be:

Your child: Mom, why did you marry Dad?

You: Why do you think?

Your child: I dunno (shrugs). You yell at him a lot so ...

You: (*Now you understand the reason for the question*) Do you think that I yell at him too much?

Your child: Maybe.

You: I'm glad you told me how you feel, because now I can work on not yelling so much at Dad. I love your dad, and that's why I married him, but I do need to work on not getting mad so much.

Here's another possible scenario:

Your child: Daddy, why did you and Mommy get married?

You: What is making you think about that right now?

Your child: Now you are getting divorced, so why did you get married in the first place?

You: Sometimes people love each other for a while, even for a long time, even long enough to have kids that they love very, very much. But then things change and the grown-ups fall out of love. It's sort of like when you have a really best friend, but then something happens and you stop being best friends—you grow apart, your interests change. It doesn't always happen though. Lots of people get married and stay married forever.

When responding to this question, it is most important to remember that you first need to understand what your child is asking. Then, be as direct, clear, and comforting as possible without offering more information than your child truly requires in order to feel satisfied.

#48: WHY ARE YOU ALWAYS SO TIRED?

Aidan (age 9) asks his mom, Deidre, every day why she is tired all the time. "I'm tired because I'm a teacher and I have three boys (ages 9, 11, and 14) who don't help all that much. I feel like I spend my entire life running from work, to the supermarket, home to make dinner, and then out to drop off and pick up my kids from activities. My husband does help when he can, but he works really long hours—he leaves around seven in the morning and often doesn't get home until eight at night or even later. Our weekends are spent going from sport to sport—among them the boys play soccer, football, hockey, baseball, lacrosse, and basketball."

I am exhausted just listening to Deidre! And I get it, I really get it—and I bet you do too. There isn't a parent I know—mom or dad, working full time, working part time, or stay-at-home—who isn't exhausted at least some of the time. So how do our kids experience our tiredness? And what does it mean to them?

Uncovering the Meaning

This question means your child notices that you are tired. On one hand, this is a good thing because it is one more indication that he is developing a greater awareness of the world beyond his own immediate needs and desires. It means that he might be becoming compassionate about the feelings of others. On the other hand, this question is different than if your child asks, "Why are you feeling tired *today*?" If he asks why you are always tired, it means he identifies you as a tired person, or as someone whose life is spent being tired, rather than as having one occasional tired day. Your child needs to make sense of this.

He recognizes that it isn't healthy to be tired all the time. After all, you teach him that he should go to bed on time so that he isn't tired in the morning, that everyone needs to get enough sleep, that one's brain and body work better when one is not tired. Since you have all but brainwashed him to recognize how important it is not to be tired, your child is searching for the reason that you are tired all the time.

Some parents are very vocal about the reasons they are tired. They talk about how much work they have, about how challenging it is to take care of their children, and how they never get a break. If you are experiencing stress and you are exhausted, it is definitely healthy to vent. However, doing so in front of your child might be emotionally harmful to him. For example, perhaps you and a friend chat while waiting for the school bus in the morning about how challenging it is to be a parent, and your child (who you think is playing ball) overhears you. Or maybe at the end of the day, you talk to your partner about what a hard day it was—stressful at work and then even more so at home with the kids—and your child (who you think is watching TV) hears the conversation. Overhearing these or similar conversations— even if they seem innocuous to you—may cause your child to feel guilty that he is the reason you are tired all the time—as if he is a burden to you. His question might be prompted by a need to hear you say something different, so he can reassure himself that it is not his fault you are exhausted.

Even if your child has never asked you this exact question, you might want to consider whether you frequently complain to or around your child about being tired because your life is so hectic. Many children bear the misplaced guilty burden of feeling that it is their fault that their parents feel stressed, exhausted, aggravated, overworked, grumpy, or miserable. It is not your child's fault. You make adult choices that allow your own and your child's life to become so busy that you are exhausted. Deidre does not have to allow her boys to play six sports—she and her husband can create limits in that area. They can also insist that their children become more actively involved in the household chores in order to alleviate some of her feeling of exhaustion. You too need to make choices so that you feel less tired (of course, this is an entire topic for another day). But until then, don't pass your feelings on to your child.

There are, of course, other reasons that you might be tired. You should regard this question as a red flag that you are not functioning at an optimal level and that you are communicating this to your child. Depression is a common cause of tiredness and wanting to sleep a lot. Depression saps one's energy, leaving you with an almost constant feeling of exhaustion. Depression can occur postpartum; it can be triggered by current or past sad or traumatic life events; it can be caused by changes in the seasons; or you can experience it for what seems like no reason at all. Some common symptoms of depression are:

- exhaustion, wanting to sleep a lot, having trouble sleeping
- sadness, crying, feeling empty

- trouble concentrating, focusing, making decisions
- feeling worthless, guilty, helpless, hopeless
- eating too much, eating too little
- loss of interest in normal activities
- headaches, stomach aches, body aches
- thinking about death, wanting to die, thinking about killing yourself, planning to kill yourself (if you have any thoughts of suicide, see a doctor or go to an emergency room *immediately*)

Other possible causes of tiredness include anemia (iron deficiency), untreated hypothyroidism, being overweight or underweight, not eating enough, or eating unhealthily. Even if you think that your tiredness is caused by the daily grind, if it seems to be getting worse or doesn't get better even when you do relax, I strongly suggest that you see your doctor to have a complete physical examination to rule out possible medical causes that may be causing or contributing to you feeling tired.

The Best Way to Respond

Your first instinct might be to say to your child, "I'm not tired; it's your imagination" (or something similar). However, by doing so, you will invalidate what he is feeling and discourage him from sharing any future concerns. A better response is to accept that, to your child, you really do appear tired and perhaps lethargic a lot of the time. Your first step is to stop and think about how you feel most of the time. Then take an objective look at your behavior. Consider how much you talk about feeling tired, exhausted, stressed, or busy, particularly in the presence of your child.

In addition, think about how much time you spend sitting or lying down, napping, resting, or relaxing, rather than playing with your kids or helping them with daily activities. Does your partner have to do "extra" to make up for what you are too tired to do?

When your child asks you this question, your primary goal is to make sure he doesn't think that he is the reason that you are tired.

For example, your response should *not* include phrases like the following:

- "I'm tired because being a mom is exhausting."
- "I'm tired because my job is hard, but I need to do it so I have enough money to buy you the things you want."
- "If I didn't have to take you to so many activities, I wouldn't be so tired."
- "If you behaved better and didn't bicker with your sister, I wouldn't be so exhausted."
- "If you and your brothers helped around the house, I'd be much less tired."

Rather, your response to him should focus on what you can do to help yourself. It might sound like the following: "It's very observant that you notice I'm often tired. Perhaps I'm not getting enough sleep or eating healthily enough. I think I will go to my doctor for a full check-up. I'm also going to start having an earlier bedtime, so that I'm not so tired during the day. I always tell you that it's important to have enough energy during the day. Well, that's true for grown-ups too."

It is very important that you take the necessary steps to address this concern. Being chronically tired will not only interfere with you being able to parent your child successfully, it will also affect you negatively in every other part of your life.

#49: WHEN I'M OLDER, CAN I BORROW YOUR SHOES/HAVE YOUR JEWELRY/ SHARE YOUR CLOTHES/USE YOUR RAZOR OR SHAMPOO?

Harriet's daughter Tia (age 9) is always asking her mom if they will be able to share Harriet's clothes when Tia is older. "Sometimes I think it's cute, but not always," explained Harriet. "She asks me so often that I wonder if she's planning a takeover!"

Many parents, like Harriet, have ambivalent feelings about this anticipated milestone. In addition, they are curious about why their children are is already thinking about it. They look forward to the time when they will be able to bond with their children around "intimate" types of sharing like clothing. However, they also worry that the boundaries will not be clear. Is this an issue to address now, or should you wait until it becomes a reality?

Uncovering the Meaning

It is interesting that your child is thinking about sharing your clothes, accessories (jewelry, watches, ties, belts, scarves), shoes, and toiletries. Other children think even further into the future. For example, some parents report that their elementary-age kids ask if, in the future, they will be able to borrow (or have) their parents' cars, briefcases, or kitchenware. The older of my daughters (age 13), who loves to cook and bake, has laid eventual claim to one of my sets of china—she told me so at least two years ago!

This question indicates that your child is beginning to think about what it will feel like to be grown up. She is wondering how it would be to wear grown up clothes or shoes or use adult toiletries or other items. She is daring to picture herself older than she is right now—in a different body, with changed needs. Wow! Pretty cool, huh?

What's more, your child is also giving you a heads-up that when she gets to this next, exciting stage, she is going to want you to be her guide, figuratively and *literally*. She is telling you that she will want you to help her "try on" her new role of growing up, by letting her borrow or have the items she will need. In other words, she wants you to equip her for her new role. In her child's mind, she perceives it sort of like playing dress-up, but for real.

Now let me give you a different, slightly psychological way of looking at this (you know me by now, I'm determined to make you a psychologist!). The items your child wants to borrow from you might function like a blankie or stuffed animal, otherwise known as a *transitional object*, helping her make the leap from childhood into adulthood, knowing that she is taking a little bit of you with her.

How do you feel about your child borrowing your clothes? Some parents are thoroughly excited at this idea—but many are not. The idea of sharing clothes, shoes, or any other personal items, even with one's own child, creates anxious or stressful feelings for a great many people. For other parents, there is already a concern that, given your child's personality, she would not take care of your possessions. For still other parents, they are not sure yet how they will feel about sharing with a child—it seems so far in the future to be making such a commitment. So how *should* you respond when confronted with this question?

The Best Way to Respond

To begin, for some parents, the need to resolve this question may not be as far into the future as you think. For example, some children's feet grow very quickly, and you may find yourself sharing a shoe size with your child by fifth or sixth grade. In addition, some items, like shampoo, jewelry, scarves, hats, ties, socks, and other small items can likely be shared right now if your child asks and if you so choose.

It is, therefore, important for you to consider how you feel about the issue of sharing. I strongly recommend that you do not humor your child by saying, "Sure, you can borrow my clothes when you're older," with no intention of following through, hoping that she won't remember. She will!

If sharing clothes, shoes, or jewelry is not something with which you are comfortable, you need to explain this to your child, making sure that you are clear that your decision has nothing to do with her. You could also explain that you may let her share some things, but not others.

Your response to the question, "When I'm older, can I borrow your clothes?" could be as follows: "When you're older, we will make sure that you have lots of cool teenage clothes that you really love so that you don't need to borrow mine. I've never really liked lending my clothes to anyone, ever since I was a little girl, so I probably won't lend you very much. But I bet we'll be able to find a couple of things for you to borrow from me when you're older. We'll talk about it then."

If you are not sure how you'll feel and you don't want to make a commitment to your child just yet, that's just fine, even if it frustrates her because she would like you to just say yes.

Another response to the question might be similar to the following: "We're going to have to wait until you're older to make that decision. By then we will know if you still like my clothes! We will also know if they fit you nicely—because we may have different shapes. I will also see how I feel about lending them to you. I've never been comfortable lending my things, since people don't always treat them well or remember to give them back. But when you're older, we'll talk about it again. I'm not saying yes, and I'm not saying no."

#50: DID YOU HAVE A HAPPY CHILDHOOD?

Julia was surprised when her daughter Ella (age 10), asked if Julia's childhood had been happy. "I wasn't really prepared to answer her," explained Julia. "I didn't have such a bad childhood, because I was loved, but it wasn't great because my father died when I was twelve, and we sort of ran out of money."

If you had a simple and perfect childhood, this question is easy to answer. But not many parents had simple and perfect childhoods. If you did, then feel free to skip this question. I won't be insulted, I promise! However, if you feel your response might be a little more complicated, then keep reading.

Uncovering the Meaning

Life is complicated. A great many parents did not have happy childhoods. Some were mediocre, and some were mostly happy with periods of sadness. And of course there are many variations—I couldn't possibly touch on them all. Where do you fit in?

Who you are as a person, and especially *as a parent*, has a great deal to do with the kind of childhood you experienced. Specifically, *the blueprint for the type of parent you are now was created from the way you were parented*. This does not mean that you are a replica of your own parents (although it might mean that). Rather, some of your parenting traits have been passed down from them. For example, if your parents yelled a lot, you are more likely to yell at your children (unless you work really hard to not yell at them). In addition—and even more importantly—the type, quality, and amount of love you received from your parents (and other people who took care of you as a child), helps formulate that parenting blueprint. For example, if your mom did not show you much affection (didn't tell you she loved you, didn't give hugs and kisses), it might be hard for you to do so with your kids—because you don't have the blueprint for it. But you can work hard to break the generational cycle and create a new blueprint by giving your child lots of hugs and kisses.

Of course, many other factors affect the way one behaves as a parent. However, barring unique circumstances, the way you were raised is probably the most powerful of all influences. It is important to keep this in mind as you are raising your own children.

Now that we understand that there is a direct relationship between your childhood and the way you parent your children, the question remains, how much should you reveal about your childhood to your child?

The Best Way to Respond

It can be tempting to "tell all," especially if you are bitter and angry with your parent. However, in *very* many cases, people behave differently as grandparents than they did as parents. In fact, at times, a sense of remorse will cause the parent of a grown child to try to make up for having been a less than adequate parent, by being very attentive (either with time or financially) to a grandchild.

In this case, responding to the question truthfully will confuse your child. The loving, caring grandparent she knows and loves doesn't seem capable of the awful things you describe. In addition, your child might feel that she has to choose sides: you or her grandparent.

Another consideration is whether you would like your child to have information that she may not be able to keep secret. Although your childhood might seem like a long time ago, if your parents are still in your life, then discussing a "bad" childhood is very much like airing dirty laundry to family and friends who know your parents, should your child blab about it. This is especially true if your current relationship with your parents is good or even reasonably good. Sharing childhood memories with your child—other than good ones—could open up old wounds and cause ill will. It is not fair or reasonable to ask an elementary-age child to keep such information a secret, so it is far better not to share such information if it might cause harm in any way.

Next, even if you do not think that talking about your sad or bad childhood experiences could harm your parents or their relationship with your child, consider the impact it might have on *your* relationship with your child. Is having this information going to make your child feel sorry for you? If so, it is not in your child's best interest to know about it. Is it going to make your child feel guilty that she has a happy childhood, but you didn't? If you are not sure, then it is better not to tell your child. Children who tend to be anxious, worriers, or who internalize their own and other people's problems are generally not those with whom you should talk about having had an unhappy childhood.

Last, it is important not to use your own unhappy childhood as leverage when disciplining your child. Beginning in elementary school it will cause enormous resentment between you and your child, which will continue through the adolescent years. For example, when trying to get your child to listen to you, you *wouldn't* want to say, "You know I didn't have a dad, and you're lucky that you have me, so the least you can do is listen when I ask you to do something." Or "Stop asking me to buy you things. When I was your age, we didn't have any money so we appreciated every little thing!"

10

One Last Question

The questions in this book offer you a very special opportunity to launch a lifetime of wonderful communication between you and your child—all you have to do is begin by answering them. However, that is just the beginning. Each time you answer a question, your child is sure to have another one, and another. I am sure you can see from the pages you have read that the way you listen, respond, and *ask more questions* is the key to becoming and staying connected with your child, now and for the rest of your and your child's lives.

My last question is for you: can you imagine what it would be like if your child did not ask you questions?

Probably not, right? I know that I definitely can't! It would be boring and mundane. It would mean that your child lacked curiosity or a yearning to learn. Without the questions, your days would not be filled with the same desire and need to challenge your child's creativity and endless drive for a changing world. How dull it would be!

For this reason, I want to ask you—implore you—to have patience with your child when he asks you so many questions that you feel like your head might explode. Remember that this is his way of learning and communicating. Don't forget that answering questions is part of the way that you can build a deep and meaningful relationship with your child. So please don't become frustrated or annoyed.

Instead, celebrate your child's questions—they give you a window into the worries and fears, through which you can help your child. They also represent achievement, intelligence, creativity, and social growth. Your child's questions are part of the fabric of her very soul. Answer them with love and respect!

About the
Author

Larry Cuocci

Dr. Susan Bartell is a nationally renowned psychologist and author who has been helping children, teens, and families lead healthier, happier lives for nearly twenty years. Dr. Susan has appeared on *Good Morning America*, *20/20*, and *The Today Show*, and is a frequent contributor to the *New York Times*, *Parenting* magazine, *Family Circle*, *WebMD*, *Women's Day*, *Nick Jr.*, and *Seventeen*.

ALSO AVAILABLE FROM
DR. SUSAN BARTELL

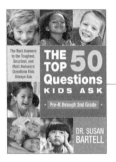